CO-AVY-495

# BEING
# BLACK
# TEACHING
# BLACK

## POLITICS AND PEDAGOGY
## IN RELIGIOUS STUDIES

EDITED BY *NANCY LYNNE WESTFIELD*

ABINGDON PRESS
NASHVILLE

BEING BLACK, TEACHING BLACK
POLITICS AND PEDAGOGY IN RELIGIOUS STUDIES

Library of Congress Cataloging-in-Publication Data

Being Black, teaching Black : politics and pedagogy in religious studies / edited by Nancy Lynne Westfield.
    p. cm.
Includes bibliographical references.
ISBN 978-0-687-46503-3 (pbk.: alk. paper)
1. Black theology.   I. Westfield, Nancy Lynne.

BT82.7.B45   2008
230.89'96073—dc22

2008008623

08 09 10 11 12 13 14 15 16 17—10 9 8 7 6 5 4 3 2 1

MANUFACTURED IN THE UNITED STATES OF AMERICA

# CONTENTS

# RESPONSES

# ACKNOWLEDGMENTS

This project has been an exhausting labor of love that has challenged all of us to think differently about the necessity of collaboration, the challenge of deep conversation, and the need for new ways of generating and producing intellectual materials that can be used in broader arenas. We are indebted to the Wabash Center for Teaching and Learning in Theology and Religion and to Dr. Lucinda Huffaker, former executive director of the center, for supporting us with a research grant as well as supporting us beyond the research phase and into this writing project. We want to thank the institutions where each of the contributors work for their willingness to free up time for us to collaborate on this project: The Theological School at Drew University, Rice University, Wilford-Laurier, Texas Christian University, Brite Divinity School at Texas Christian University, Claremont School of Theology, and Presbyterian School of Theology in Louisville. We want to thank the Reverend Elizabeth Jones, former student at Drew Theological, who managed the budget and program aspects of the project. Her attention to detail and hospitality made our research happen. We thank our colleagues, Carolyn M. Jones, Boyung Lee, and Charles Foster, from whom we have written responses to our work. Your words, work, critique, and solidarity are vitally important to us. And most of all, we are thankful to the ancestors on whose shoulders we stand, for their inspiration and perseverance. We acknowledge, without their struggle, sacrifice, and unwavering faith, we would not have the freedom or responsibility of grappling with these critical issues. We say to the babies yet to be born that this is but one sample of our faithfulness to you.

# INTRODUCTION

## *Nancy Lynne Westfield*

ow much does race matter in the politics of the United States, in the classrooms of higher education and theological education, in the lives of teachers, learners, and their families? What does it mean to the dynamics of the classroom when teachers and students are from different races? What happens when the professor is Black? As I pen these introductory remarks, news headlines are ripe with racial and racialized incidents: racist, sexist, and vulgar statements made by shock jock Don Imus against the women's basketball team of Rutgers University; the elite, white, male lacrosse team at Duke University and their role in the alleged rape of an African American female student from North Carolina State University who worked a campus party as a stripper; Barack Obama and his candidacy for president—the questions surrounding his run for office are asking if people will follow a Black man, and is he Black enough?—the Virginia Tech massacre by a Korean American student—the list could go on. The conflicts fueled by racial difference and the challenges of racial diversity are alive in the national arena, and they are equally alive in higher education classrooms. We contend that issues of race influence the dynamics of higher education classrooms in ways that educational leaders and administrators have yet to take seriously. The contributors to this anthology are scholars in seminaries and departments of religion, but we are suggesting that the issues we raise are germane to all of higher education, regardless of the discipline or type of postsecondary institution.

# INFLUENCES OF BLACK FACULTY

The number of racial-ethnic scholars in the academy is on the rise, and the number of African American scholars teaching in seminaries is also on the rise.[1] Further, we know that theological education takes place beyond the context of seminaries and includes colleges and universities through religious studies. There have, no doubt, been some noteworthy conversations about the influence of Black scholars on the academy and on theological education. James Cone's 2001 keynote address at the American Academy of Religion's annual meeting gives credence to this observation. Professor Cone chided the white academy for overlooking and relegating Black scholars. Though his keynote was significant, recent conversations have been brief and scattered. Institutions have been transformed by the work of faculty members such as Cone, Delores Williams, Peter Paris, Gayraud Wilmore, and Jacquelyn Grant. The significance of their contribution is marked by the fact that the overwhelming majority of religion and theological programs teach liberation theology in their required introductory courses. Further, most liberation theologies, such as Minjung, Womanist, Mujerista, or Black theology, credit Cone and African American liberation theologies with being largely responsible for their development. An example of this development is the work of Ada Maria Isasi-Diaz, the progenitor of mujerista theology.[2] However, a strong case can be made that there is no evidence that primarily white institutions have reflected on the implications of the presence of African American students and faculty for understanding and planning theological education and religious studies. It has seemed as though white institutions have recruited Black scholars to placate the challenges of Black students and Black churches, if and when Black students are enrolled. Furthering the problem, Black scholars are overwhelmed with the demands of being pastors and community organizers, along with their responsibilities as scholars and teachers. The multiple demands placed on Black faculty from multiple arenas of accountability leave them little time to reflect on the meaning and significance of their presence in theological and religious education. Too little reflection has been done concerning the contributions, influences, and roles of Black faculty in religious and theological education in predominantly white institutions concerning intellectual contributions, pedagogical contributions, or institutional enhancement.

## ILL-PREPARED FOR DIVERSITY

Few persons would dispute the devastating prevalence of racism and sexism in U.S. society. The prejudices, bigotry, and oppressive forces that are operational in the larger society do not somehow vanish or lose their power in the higher-education classroom. Classrooms are not politically neutral, nor are they politically benign. On the contrary, the politics of the larger society permeates the academic arena and saturates the classroom. The biases, prejudices, and cultural insensitivities that exist in the larger society are brought to bear on our classrooms. Classrooms steeped in the assumptions of domination are classrooms of discomfort and pain for teacher and learner alike. For a classroom in the U.S. context where the professor is an African American, issues of classism, racism, and sexism and other hegemonic practices of exclusion and domination are present and operative—sometimes in lethal doses.

Classrooms in the United States are becoming increasingly racially diverse while little preparing the students, teachers, or institutions for this change. While some schools will provide the occasional workshop on diversity or have been thoughtful about curricular issues for white students in making them more aware of issues affecting non-whites, few institutions have conceived of or accomplished major changes for accommodating the needs of and adapting to the obstacles that arise for non-white teachers and learners. Not only have institutions not changed in major ways, little effort is given to assisting learners and teachers with orienting and preparing for the newness they will encounter in each other. Diversity creates new dynamics in classroom interactions and requires that white students cope with situations for which they are ill-prepared, and likewise requires Black faculty to survive hostile classrooms. Diversity in classrooms requires new relationships, new metaphors for making sense of reality, and new ways of thinking old thoughts; little of this need for innovation, reorientation, and change has been considered.

Further exacerbating the problem is the adult learner. By the time a learner gets to college, seminary, and graduate school, he or she has gained a level of academic proficiency. Often those students who become professors are unwilling or unable to "relearn" how to be students in diverse classrooms where their authority is challenged, their privileged roles are critiqued—where there is little frame of reference on succeeding and "passing this course." Regardless of whether students resist or participate in this relearning, the diverse classroom and the ensuing dynamics become a place of unfamiliarity for the learners and unplanned surprise for the teachers.

The chapters of this anthology explore, analyze, and illumine some of the dynamics in the academy that occur when the professor is Black. In many instances, the presence of a Black faculty person in a white institution is what constitutes diversity in the classroom. In other cases, Black faculty are confronted with frustrated, ill-equipped, and angry students from multiple backgrounds. Regardless of the kind of diversity, there is a disruption of pedagogy that is all too often burdensome for teacher and learner. While African American scholars are not surprised when we encounter racist, classist, and sexist attitudes and behaviors in our own classrooms, we are still wounded by these attacks. The violence of racism and sexism takes a toll on even the most stalwart of warriors. The racist and sexist reality of higher education can dampen and even snuff out the passion for teaching and for learning.

## WHO SHOULD READ THIS BOOK AND WHY?

We hope that people who take higher education seriously will read this book. For us, this includes professors of all races, administrators in a variety of school settings, and learners who have made the commitment to humanizing relational pedagogies and who see and feel the frustration of attempting these pedagogies in diverse settings. We also hope students will read this book as co-teachers and co-learners realizing that schools, especially classrooms, are the responsibility of teacher *and* learner.

Those of us who have participated in this research and writing are well aware that the issues we raise concerning the dynamics of raced and gendered classrooms do not belong exclusively to Black professors. We understand that this reality of struggle and confusion belongs to many other groups of colleagues. We know that non-white people who are not of African descent contend with similar struggles of oppression and alienation. While we are aware of this general phenomenon at work, we are focusing upon the particularity of the experience of African American professors who find ourselves constantly under siege by the racist, sexist, alienating dynamics in our own classrooms and educational settings. We hope that our effort to critically reflect upon our particular experiences will encourage others to reflect upon their experiences. It is our hope that this text will spark a much-needed dialogue concerning the dynamics of classrooms when race, class, and gender seem to have created insurmountable challenges to teaching and learning.

We suspect that this conversation will be useful to white academic institutions that do not yet know how to most effectively support racial ethnic and minority faculty toward scholarly excellence. The inability to effectively support their faculty may be the result of African American scholars' failure to clearly articulate their role outside of criticizing racism, or it may simply be due to white resistance to making substantial changes in their approach to higher education in general, and to theological education, specifically. We also see a use for this text in predominately Black institutions where differences in gender, sexual orientation, and class pose pedagogical challenges. Issues of race, politics, and identity must be grappled with if we are to make effective changes in educational arenas of the twenty-first century.

## OVERVIEW OF THE ANTHOLOGY

The research that informs these essays was made possible by a grant from Wabash Center for Teaching and Learning in Theology and Religion. The grant allowed us to gather as researchers over two years, using a case study methodology, to grapple with issues of diversity, politics, and identity. We intentionally designed a project that convened a conversation enriched by our multiple experiences and our wide career development. We believe, though we are a research group of theology and religion scholars, that the issues we discuss are farther reaching than seminaries and graduate departments of religion. Our central research questions were, What does it mean to be a Black scholar/pedagogue—must you teach Black? Is there a Black hermeneutic, or are we just as white as our colleagues? Are there particular teaching practices used by Black faculty that enhance, sabotage, or challenge the lessons for our students?

Many of the scenarios recounted in this anthology will seem ridiculous, even laughable. Some readers will say that these events happen to every teacher, regardless of race, at some time in his or her career. We do not think so. Or, readers will likely say that the professor brought many of these encounters upon himself or herself by the way in which he or she interacted with the students or colleagues. Painfully, we discovered in our conversation and research that these racist and demeaning events were regular occurrences—too numerous to mention in this anthology. We contend that we had little control to initiate, temper, or avoid the incidents due to the oppressive nature of the circumstance. Many of the critical moments happened unprovoked and were startling—leaving the Black professor feeling as if he or she had survived a drive-by shooting. We assure you that the critical incidents that we recount and reflect upon are actual events with the names and other identifying information changed to protect the privacy of those involved. We are not claiming victim status. We are not recounting these stories to titillate or shock. We acknowledge the vulnerability in recounting and analyzing these stories. As scholars and teachers who are deeply invested in improving and healing the academy, we offer our stories and our critique so that we all may move toward a healthier way of being the academy.

## THE QUESTIONS WE GRAPPLE WITH

The essays of this anthology reflect collaborative efforts as well as individual thinking and personal reflection. As the research was a series of collaborative gathering, you will see that our conversations were influential to our thinking, resulting in, for some of the essays, similar themes and resonance in some of our arguments and reflections. You will also see, as a result of our collaboration, significant ideas that are independent and that stand on their own merit. Seven of the essays are written by individual authors and two of the essays are coauthored. The coauthored essays introduce and analyze an innovative model for teaching, which is being developed at Drew Theological Seminary.

Carol Duncan's essay, "Visible/Invisible: Teaching Popular Culture and the Vulgar Body in Black Religious Studies," grapples with questions such as, In what ways can cultural texts that include aspects of the "vulgar" be incorporated into curricula that include popular culture? How are Black women teachers' subjectivities and bodies implicated in the teaching of popular cultural texts, especially those that involve the vulgar, given racial and sexual hierarchies that position Black women in popular culture as mammies and jezebels?

Arthur L. Pressley, author of "Using Novels of Resistance to Teach Intercultural Empathy and Cultural Analysis," engages the questions, Why is there a growing resistance to African American teachers even as the country becomes more diverse? Why does the presence of an African American, male professor cause students to assume that the intellectual material of the course is irrelevant? What would it mean for students to see Black, male professors as role models and professional exemplars?

"E-Racing While Black," by Stephen G. Ray Jr., confronts the following questions: How do educators understand the idea of the "racialized imagination" and its relationship to theological education? What particular challenges do Black theological educators face in trying to teach past this imagination, in other words to /e-race/ the faith? What pedagogical practices are available to accomplish the work of /e-racing/ teaching about the Christian faith?

Nancy Lynne Westfield, author of "Called Out My Name or Had I Known You Were Somebody: The Pain of Fending Off Stereotypes," reflects struggles with such questions as, What experiences of racism and sexism in the theological classroom are most debilitating, paralyzing, death-dealing to Black women faculty, and why? What if racism and sexism are disrupters of pedagogy in a Black woman's classroom? What is the cost of this disruption to her personally, spiritually, and professionally?

In "Reading the Signs: The Black Body as Non-Written Text," Anthony B. Pinn asks the questions, What is the implicit and explicit significance of the body within the classroom? How might the presence of the physical body impact pedagogical considerations, particularly when the bodies are Black?

Lincoln Galloway, in his "Black Rhythms and Consciousness: Authentic Being and Pedagogy," grapples with the question, What is authentically Black? What does "being Black" mean for our existence as humans and our vocation as teachers? What kinds of pedagogies emerge when one is Black? What particular rhythms of consciousness give meaning to teaching and learning?

Stacey Floyd-Thomas, author of "From Embodied Theodicy to Embodied Theos," raises the following contestable ethical issues: What does it mean for Black, women professors to claim authority and respectability in the classroom while refusing to be seen as Mammy (Mother Confessor) or Whore (Temptress)? What happens when, even before she utters her first word in a classroom, her Black female body is the most contested and embattled aspect of the teaching-learning experience? To what extent are Black women's bodies the proverbial battlefields for the so-called "culture wars" in this society, and how can a cease-fire be declared?

The coauthored chapters each focus on an innovative project at Drew Theological Seminary called "God-Talk with Black Thinkers," comanaged by Arthur L. Pressley and Nancy Lynne Westfield. "Teaching Black: God-Talk with Black Thinkers," authored by the same colleagues, engages the questions, What does it mean for a Black student to learn about issues of faith, theology, and leadership in a white institution? What type of curriculum prepares Black seminarians to be effective and competent in the local church? And the essay "Emancipatory Historiography as Pedagogical Praxis: The Blessing and the Curse of Theological Education for the Black Self and Subject," written by Juan Floyd-Thomas and Stacey Floyd-Thomas, asks, What does it mean for Black faculty persons to teach toward assisting Black students in overcoming the perceived conundrum described by Carter Woodson of the blessing and curse of Blackness? What might the development of an experimental model of pedagogical praxis that strives to engage, empower, and ultimately emancipate Black students look like and what are the challenges and pitfalls of the model?

We thought it vitally important, given the racial particularity of this text, to get responses from colleagues who were not part of the research and who have written on similar topics. As she is a senior female African American scholar, we asked Carolyn M. Jones for critique. She is Associate Professor of Religion and Literature, African American Religions and Literatures, Religious Theory and Thought, Women's Spirituality and Writings in the Department of Religion, University of Georgia. As a junior female Korean American scholar, Boyung Lee's response was also invited. Boyung Lee is Assistant Professor of Educational Ministries, Pacific School of Religion. And we are pleased to have a response from white senior scholar Charles Foster, Professor Emeritus of Religion and Education, Candler School of Theology, Emory University, and mentor of Nancy Lynne Westfield.

And finally, a word about why the terms *Black* and *African American* are used interchangeably in this text. The first reason is the simple reality that we live in a historical moment in which there are significant numbers of people in our society to whom these terms were central to their identity formation and the larger politics of racial formation within our culture. We assess the matter to be much like that of an earlier era, when the terms *Negro* and *Colored* were used interchangeably to refer to persons and communities of African descent. In our estimation, it would be a poor pedagogical practice to gloss over this reality. On a deeper level, the contributors and I wish to acknowledge the political and scholarly dimensions of this decision. We use these terms interchangeably because the fluidity of their use in the vernacular of communities of African descent mark the multiple ways that persons of dark-hued skin and African ancestry have creatively engaged in identity formation in the midst of being systemically oppressed and summarily labeled as inferior. It is our assessment that the self-referential use of these terms by persons and communities of African descent has signaled a steadfast refusal to be defined by pejorative assessments. By claiming and reinterpreting what began as terms of derision and using them fluidly, Black persons and communities are expressing an agency that simplistic labeling would deny. Our employment of these terms interchangeably is a reflection of this enactment of communal agency and an affirmation of the dynamism of the tradition and heritage that we are part and parcel of while we struggle to teach in this foreign land known as the academy. We employ the terms interchangeably as a gesture that we do not stand outside of this tradition, but we stand as thinking people who are members of the tradition and who are wholeheartedly making use of scholarship as a gesture of resistance and liberation. The interchangeable use of these terms is typical in Womanist scholarship, Black studies, and African American studies. We believe words and ideas are powerful elements in the struggle for liberation. To that end, we have chosen to write the term *white* in lowercase and to capitalize *Black* and *African American* as a signal of rhetorical disruption of domination and white supremacy.

VIEWS
VIEWS
VIEWS
VIEWS
VIEWS
VIEWS
**VIEWS**
VIEWS
VIEWS
VIEWS
VIEWS
VIEWS
VIEWS
VIEWS
VIEWS
VIEWS
VIEWS

# Visible/Invisible

## TEACHING POPULAR CULTURE AND THE VULGAR BODY IN BLACK RELIGIOUS STUDIES

### Carol B. Duncan

*In what ways can cultural texts which include aspects of the vulgar be incorporated into curricula which includes popular culture? How are Black women teachers' subjectivities and bodies implicated in the teaching of popular cultural texts, especially those which involve the vulgar, given racial and sexual hierarchies which position black women in popular culture as mammies and jezebels?*

The body is surrounded by an atmosphere of certain uncertainty. . . . And I was battered down by tom-toms, cannibalism, intellectual deficiency, fetishism, racial defects . . . I took myself far off from my own presence. . . . What else could it be for me but an amputation, an excision, a hemorrhage that spattered my whole body with Black blood?[1]

P rofessor Duncan, what does *motherfucker* mean?" The question was asked of me, a few years ago, by a white male student, as I delivered a lecture on oral traditions of the African Diaspora to an undergraduate class. The question took me by surprise even though I had long ago, in my teaching practice, relinquished the notion of being able to predict what was going to happen on any given day in the classroom. As a university teacher, in fact, I have made it an established part of my teaching practice to invite students' questions and comments as an integral component of the classroom learning experience. This invitation to question, comment, and dialogue, however, is couched within a framework of relations in which mutual respect and responsibility are paramount. This particular question did not seem to be paying attention to these ground rules of classroom communication. I was taken aback by the question and the way in which it was asked: frank, bold, and with no warning or acknowledgment that a "curse word" was about to be uttered, thus taking the talk of the classroom outside of its usual context. The student had interrupted the lecture to ask the question. In posing it, he situated his curiosity about the term with his love of hip-hop culture and rap music in particular, noting that he had always wondered about the meaning of this particular term that proliferated in the recordings of rap artists whom he admired. In his iteration of the question, he used the word *motherfucker* several times, seeming to relish, from my standpoint as listener, the actual enunciation of the word, out in the open, out loud and in the classroom. The word seemed to hang in the air, defiantly proclaiming its arrival in the conversation of the class. With its utterance, the classroom dynamic suddenly shifted and changed as the other students watched and waited to see how I would respond. Ignoring the question and carrying on as if it had not entered the room was not an option.

In the room of nearly fifty students, the majority of whom were white, I felt as if I was suddenly positioned, by this question, as an expert on all things Black, an experience that I had encountered before as a student beginning high school. I anticipated from personal experience and anecdotal conversations with other persons of African descent that being asked to take on the role of the Black expert could mean being asked to expound on any number of topics from various African and African Diasporan cultural traditions and historical epochs. This occurs because the positioning as expert in this context presumes a sameness of Blackness and Black experience that is shared across linguistic, geographical, cultural, religious, and even temporal locations. The assumed expertise is not based on scholarly study or training but on life experience. Encountering it in the classroom, therefore, brings my location as a scholar, teacher, and expert by virtue of academic training and research into an uncomfortable juxtaposition with the underlying stereotypical assumption of Black expert knowledge based on a presumed shared cultural Blackness. My own experience in being positioned in this role, for example, had run the gamut from assumed expertise on playing basketball to southern African American cuisine, even though I, myself, am from a Caribbean background and have never played basketball or cooked southern African American foods. Black expertise, at that moment, did not involve the basketball court or the kitchen, however, but invoked another arena of Blackness: the mythical streets of urban America as the locale of hip-hop and rap cultures.

I decided that I would answer the question within the scholarly framework of the course by locating the term within the performative tradition of some genres of rap music, which used swearing and profanity for emphasis. I also noted that while the term could be used pejoratively, it could also be used affirmatively, depending on the context and the speaker and qualifying adjectives such as "bad" with an inverse meaning of "good" or "excellent." The strategy proved effective in bridging the gap between the student's question and the way in which it was posed, the apparent titillation in its utterance, and furthering the knowledge of the student, in particular, and the class as a whole.

And yet, I could not help wondering at the end of the class, as I have on other occasions when positioned as "Black expert," what was it about the course content, the classroom space, and, specifically, myself as a teacher, that occasioned the opening of the space to

6 profane language, or imagery, in a way that clearly, in my mind, went against the grain of the established relations of communication within the classroom? Was the asking of the question rude and indirectly aimed at me? Was he calling me a motherfucker by asking the question, in public, in front of the rest of the class? In asking the question, was he assuming scholarly expertise or knowledge from a presumed experientially based, stereotypical, urban Black life represented through the lens of popular cultural images in film, music video, and television of U.S.-based inner-city, Black life lived away from the classroom? These questions, admittedly, are my own and reveal my anxieties and concerns about race, gender, and class relations in the classroom.

In teaching popular culture, including music, film, and fashion that emerge from Black cultural contexts, in religious studies courses in the Canadian and American academy,[2] I have experienced interactions, such as the one described above, in which popular cultural texts, and expressions associated with them, their producers and consumers, and the very sociocultural and historical contexts in which they have emerged, are considered salacious and rude—in a word, vulgar. Their vulgarity, however, renders them both titillating and potential sites of sustained critical attention in the religious studies classroom. Similarly, my own embodiment and identity as a Black woman is implicated in the dynamic of teaching such material in classroom and larger university and community contexts that are predominantly "white." In this instance, the impact of the larger cultural reading of Black bodies as embodying or signifying rudeness, vulgarity, and transgression is implicated here. Addressing these issues of identity and social relations in the classroom is undoubtedly messy but also promises to open a space for discussion and learning that can be transformative for teachers and students.

This chapter will discuss the "the vulgar body" in the teaching of Black religious studies through examining its significance in both popular cultural texts in the classroom and the relationship of these texts to my own embodiment and identity as a Black woman teacher in the classroom. With reference to specific examples drawn from my teaching experiences, the essay problematizes the intersection of the vulgar body, in particular the vulgar body as Black and female, in the teaching of popular cultural texts suggesting that exploration of the tension between loving and desire for the vulgar Black body is a necessary part of critical pedagogy for teaching Black popular culture in a religious studies context. It is not without trepidation that I share these stories for they are not heroic teaching stories. These are stories in which my vulnerability in the classroom was made very apparent to me and probably, also, to my students, as well. Rather than having an authoritative teacherly presence, these experiences are ones in which the authenticity of my identity in the classroom was challenged in subtle and not so subtle ways. I am sharing these stories out of my love for teaching and working with students in the often challenging but extremely rewarding terrain of teaching Black popular culture in a religious studies context that is complicated by my embodiment as a Black woman.

In exploring this dynamic, this chapter discusses the problem of erasure and hypervisibility that I have experienced as a Black woman university teacher through using two "counterstories"[3] from the classroom. Experiences of student-teacher interaction in the classroom, my office, and other university spaces in which I am either completely erased in my identity as teacher-scholar or my race and gender as a Black woman are made hypervisible in stereotypical ways. In many of these experiences, both my visibility as a radically racialized and sexed and gendered Other and invisibility as a teacher-scholar occur simultaneously. The result is that I am both erased as a teacher-scholar and made hypervisible as a Black woman through stereotypic lenses that make my presence in the university classroom incongruous, if not impossible, in the context of the student-teacher interaction. Theodorea Regina Berry refers to this problematic as one of multidimensionality:

It's always something (what the fuck?). As a woman of color, some facet of my multidimensional being is always a problem, a dilemma for someone. My social status in my personal, community, cultural, and professional spheres is causing fatigue to my fatigue to my psyche. But I can't change who I am. And I won't.[4]

Like Berry, I am not prepared to relinquish my multidimensionality in the context of my work as a teacher and scholar in the academy. My analysis of the phenomenon of visibility/hypervisibility suggests that "returning of the gaze"[5] is a necessary strategy for proclaiming a self-defined and multidimensional subjectivity and humanity in what are often highly depersonalized interactions.

## THE VULGAR BODY

Literary studies scholar and cultural critic Carolyn Cooper, in her study *Noises in the Blood*,[6] described what she called the "vulgar body" in Jamaican popular culture. Cooper focused, specifically, on the genre of popular music known as dancehall, which has become popularized in international contexts beyond Jamaica since the early 1980s. As conceptualized by Cooper, the "vulgar body" includes stylistic practices, representations as well as verbal utterances. "Vulgarity" in this sense is linked to representations of Black bodies that are overtly sexualized, associated with (illicit) pleasure, and resistant to status quo moral regulation. My discussion of the teaching of the vulgar in Black religious studies contexts draws on Cooper's conceptualization and discussion. While Cooper's discussion is concerned with Jamaican dancehall culture, in particular, my discussion extends her ideas to address the teaching of hip-hop culture in music, film, and video in the religious studies classroom. Important in this regard is that, coincidentally, these texts that include Caribbean and African American musical genres such as dancehall, rap, and hip-hop, and their related cultural practices in dance and fashion, are precisely the ones that have had a major impact on contemporary youth cultures and enjoy enormous popularity internationally.[7]

In her discussion of the place of Black women in the academy, Baszile discusses the significance of Saartije Baartman's positioning as the Hottentot Venus.[8] A Khoi Khoi woman who was born in what is now South Africa at the end of the eighteenth century, Baartman was dubbed the Hottentot Venus and exhibited naked to audiences in England and France in the early nineteenth century. The focus for the public was her buttocks and genitalia. These continued to be sites of fascination even after her death as her body was dissected and her pelvis was displayed in various exhibits as late as the latter part of the twentieth century in Paris. Her remains were returned to South Africa for burial only in 2002. Baszile notes that the violence visited on Baartman's body has "forever situated the Black woman's body as abnormal and problematic."[9] She then further questions the ways in which Black women's academic work would be shaped by their embodiment by asking: "So what does it mean to live in this body, to be in the world and to conceive of the world through this body, to teach and write through this body, which without question situates Black women in academia as counterhegemonic texts?"[10] Thus, Baszile suggests that Black women's experiences are fundamentally ones shaped by spaces in between categories:

> As Black women, we live at the nexus of race and gender hierarchies; we be in the spaces in between not quite here and not quite there. We are/we be in between Black and White, male and female, and even race and gender as categories that contradict in the defining of Black women's identities.[11]

For Baszile, this "ontoepistemological in-between" status allows Black women a perspective that challenges normative associations or "reifications of Blackness around maleness," gender around whiteness, and "intellectualism around white maleness."[12] She notes that Black women in the academy who claim this in-between space from which they theorize and practice often do so in ways that run counter to the academic establishment, and the definition of knowledge is framed in racist and patriarchal ways.[13] One of the ways in which Black women have engaged this ontoepistemological in-between perspective is through the use of "The Word."[14] "The Word" here is understood as "a form of praxis in which pedagogy, scholarship, and struggle are intimately intertwined; a way of teaching and doing scholarship that embraces duality, subjectivity, and narrative in our attempts to authorize our voices."[15] "Counterstories" are one of the practices in which "The Word" is employed. "Counterstories," as a form of "oppositional scholarship," are characterized by their complexity and embrace of multiple dimensions of Black women's experiences encompassing race, gender, class, and sexuality as social relations of power.[16] In the following, I offer two examples of counterstories from the classroom in an effort to explore the dynamic of visibility and invisibility as a Black woman teacher in a religious studies classroom.

### Counterstory 1: Making Breakfast

The first example concerns my interaction with a white male student early in my teaching career. This student insisted on eating, very conspicuously, in class during my first semester of teaching. Many students consume snacks and drink coffee during morning classes; however, the nature of this consumption—the quantity, loudness, along with the student's consistently late arrival for each class—marked his practice as qualitatively different. Always arriving five to ten minutes late for each class of the biweekly introductory course, this student habitually positioned himself near the front of the class and proceeded to eat. Loudly. At first it was crisp cookies removed one by one from their rustling, plastic wrapping as I lectured. At other times he ate crunchy apples throughout the lecture. Each class, I hoped that his seemingly endless hunger would be satiated and that the snacking would be, if not brief, at least soft-sounding. Maybe he could eat something such as yogurt, through which teeth would easily slide. But this was not to be. The snacks grew larger and larger and seemingly crispier and crunchier with each class. Finally, by the fourth week of the twelve-week term, he arrived with a huge rucksack on his back and, as usual, was ten minutes late for the class. He took his, by now, customary seat near the front of the class and proceeded to methodically remove a family-sized box of cereal, a quart of milk, a ceramic bowl, and a stainless steel spoon, clanking the latter, as he did so, against the side of the bowl.

I could no longer employ the strategy of ignoring this latest and more intense act of what I had considered, by now, disrespect or disregard for my teaching and for the learning process of the other students in the class. I stopped the lecture and directly addressed him, saying, "Come on, man, you can't do that." His response, pausing as he was about to pour his cereal, was "Do what?" He was disavowing that what was taking place was, in fact, taking place. I then continued, "Preparing breakfast and eating it while I teach. I'd like you to stop." I continued by noting that his breakfast preparation and eating was seriously disrupting my teaching. He stared back at me for a few moments and then nodded his head as he put away his cereal, milk, ceramic bowl, and stainless steel spoon. I then continued with my lecture. After the class, another white male student told me that he was glad that I had spoken up since, although he had noticed this student's disruptive behavior centered around eating throughout the previous three weeks of class, he had not known what to do about it.

## Counterstory 2: Will the Real Professor Please Stand Up?

A second example involves a white male student's confession to me at the end of a course for which he had missed the first two classes of the term because he had left each time he saw me arrive and write my name on the board. His assumption was that I was a secretary who was writing the name of the professor, "Carol

Duncan," on the board in order to inform students that the professor was not coming to class that day. When he saw the same Black woman arrive for the third class and proceed to write the name "Carol Duncan" on the board yet again, he had decided to stick around to find out what arrangements the department had made for what was shaping up to be a serious absenteeism problem for Professor Duncan at the start of term. When he stayed for the class, he then found out that I was indeed Professor Duncan.

This student was not bound to tell me this story and, in fact, I would never have been the wiser about his thoughts and perceptions of my presence in the classroom during the first two weeks of the semester, were it not for his confession, about my mistaken (to him) identity. He felt compelled to let me in on his assumption since the course had been a valuable learning experience for him, and a part of that learning was having his own assumptions challenged about who teachers were in the classroom. He noted, too, that he would have felt as if he was somehow "getting away with something" and "cheating," given his opinion about my presence in the classroom, which placed me outside of the classroom context as a non-teacher, at the beginning of the semester.

## MAKING THE INVISIBLE VISIBLE

Both of these experiences that I have related involve my identity and authentic presence as a scholar-teacher in the classroom being challenged and questioned. In the first instance, the student who insisted on loud and conspicuous eating used the food and its consumption and preparation, in the last instance, to assert his presence over and above mine in the classroom. While he did not raise his voice, he imposed his presence through other types of sound—namely rustling packages and loud chewing—to challenge my presence as teacher in this classroom. Lest my assumptions be relegated solely to speculation, our verbal interchange when I confronted the behavior confirmed this dynamic. In the second instance, the student had made up a story about why a Black woman would be in the classroom writing her name on the blackboard because his previous teaching and learning experiences did not allow him to think that this woman could be the course professor.

Another dynamic highlighted by these experiences is the challenge to the authenticity of Black women teachers in the classroom. In the instance of the breakfast-eating student, he used food and its preparation to challenge my authenticity as a professor in the classroom, not just at one moment but throughout the class by using a competing sound—eating—against my voice lecturing. His eating also suggested that his food and not my lecture was his focal point. It was as if I were a live television show that he was watching as entertainment or background while he enjoyed his real focus—his meal. In the second instance, the student's perception did not allow him to even conceive of the possibility of a Black woman—any Black woman—having authority as a professor. His confession was, I saw, a ritual enactment retroactively granting me authority status as professor from the beginning of the course in order to redeem himself and the way in which he had perceived me during those introductory classes. It was also a transgressive moment in which the student was able to challenge and come to terms with sexist and racist assumptions that he was unaware that he held.

## EYE CONTACT: RETURNING THE GAZE

In her study of encounters between dominant groups and subordinate ones in classrooms and courtrooms in Canada, historian Sherene Razack, in drawing on the work of Frantz Fanon, notes the depersonalization that marks these encounters.[17] According to Fanon, in *Black Skin, White Masks*, the colonized subject is trapped in the gaze of the colonizer. The Other, in this instance, knows itself only through the lens of the colonized. This notion echoes

DuBois' suggestion of the "double consciousness" that characterizes Black American subjectivity.[18] Razack's project aims to move toward a breaking of this gaze for female subjects of color. Razack uses the notion of "looking white people in the eye," the title of her study, to challenge the notion that moments of interaction between whites and non-whites are somehow outside of history and therefore manageable by strategies of sensitivity.[19] Her argument here is that communications are historically and socially constructed. Thus, in the examples that I have relayed, I suspect that historically constructed raced and gendered social relations of power played a large role in shaping the quality of the interactions between the two male students and me.

Looking these students in the eye and returning the gaze was an important strategy in reshaping the dynamics of these encounters so that they could be places of transformative learning. In doing so, I challenged what my colleague Nancy Lynne Westfield[20] has noted as the "surreal" aspect of these relations, which are echoed in students coming to my office with my name clearly printed on the sign outside and asking me when Professor Duncan will return. The assumption here is that even though all indicators point to my being Professor Duncan, gendered and sexed stereotypes render my actually occupying my office as a professor an impossibility. The surrealism of these encounters rests in the extent to which stories are constructed to explain seemingly ordinary situations such as my sitting in my office to meet with students, writing my name on the board, and teaching my classes. The stories always require considerable inventiveness and ignore what might seem like the obvious. In effect, they render a kind of casual violence to our psyches as Black women teacher-scholars. As Himani Bannerji, a South Asian Canadian-based sociologist and writer notes: "The social relations of teaching and learning are relations of violence for us, those who are not white, who teach courses on 'Gender, Race, and Class,' to a 'white' body of students in a 'white' university. I want to hide from this gaze."[21] But we cannot hide from the gaze. We must look back at it and in doing so confront the distorted reflections of ourselves. This is the basis of a womanist pedagogy that takes seriously the context as well as content of teaching and learning in the academy. Every moment, is, in effect, a possibility of transformation both for ourselves and for our students.

My experiences illustrate that in our daily lives as Black women teachers, our individual and collective "fact of Blackness," to use Fanon's term, can appear in the seemingly mundane and routine occurrences of our everyday professional lives to remind us that we are indeed engaged in the extraordinary as Black woman teacher-scholars, each and every day. As sociologist Dorothy E. Smith reminds us, "The everyday world is problematic"[22] and it is in the interstices of our daily professional lives that we encounter and challenge dominant power relations.

# Using Novels of Resistance to Teach Intercultural Empathy and Cultural Analysis

## Arthur L. Pressley

*Why is there a growing resistance to African American teachers, even as the country becomes more diverse? What does it mean to teach so that students learn to move meaningfully between multiple cultural worlds? Why do students refuse to be influenced by Black, male professors who are experts in their fields?*

## COUNTERINTUITIVE REALITY

Strange as it may sound, the more diverse the United States becomes, the more students seem to struggle with accepting African American teachers. While white students are resistant, many African American students as well as other students of color also are part of this group. I am aware this observation seems counterintuitive. The logical and natural assumption would be that the more culturally and racially diverse a faculty, the more open and accepting the educational systems would be toward Black leadership and teachers. It is logical to think that the decimation and deconstruction of the "good old boy" political machine would yield educational systems that are politically receptive to Black faculty and administrators. One would think that students of color, and women especially, would desire a faculty who represented, by their very presence, a challenge to the traditional order. It would be normal to assume that students would long for Black faculty whose social location might incline them to bring new perspectives and questions to extant theories. Instead, the opposite has happened. Students, Black and non-Black, have growing hesitancy to accept mentoring from Black faculty even while acknowledging that some Black persons are great teachers. Why is there a growing resistance to African American teachers, even as the country becomes more diverse?

## BALKANIZATION IN THE USA

Increased cultural and ethnic diversity has caused a shift in the structure and goals of education and with it a growing resentment toward Black faculty. In part, this is a result of the manner in which this diversity now takes place in the United States. The increased diversity has been the result of an immigration pattern quite different from previous generations. Previously, immigrants to the United States sought, to a larger extent, to become acculturated into the larger society. In contrast, current immigrant communities maintain the primacy of their own cultural traits for individuals and for their wider ethnic community. When economic rather than political forces are the catalyst and determinant for immigration, the immigrant people seek to maintain their cultural identity rather than choose acculturation. Social scientists refer to this as a "balkanization" of American immigration patterns.[1] This metaphor refers to Yugoslavian social patterns where diverse immigrant communities sought to live in distinct and separate communities without melding into one nation. Growing numbers of theorists feel that similar patterns are beginning to emerge in the United States. Some theorists argue that the term *balkanization* may be an overstatement, not because the term is inaccurate but because they fear further overreaction to the growing presence of immigrants by the established citizen population. After the 2006 congressional elections, some theorists concluded that it was the immigration issue, not the war in the Middle East, that gave the Democratic Party control of Congress. Even if this conclusion cannot be proved, it points to growing fear over the new immigrant patterns in the United States.

# THE MATRIX OF RACISM

With this growing population of immigrants joining into a nation of immigrants, the matrix of racism against Blackness remains the eternal symbol for powerlessness, poverty, and victimization. The constant factor in U.S. immigration patterns has been that no one wants to be identified with Blackness. This is an attitude brought to the United States, intensified once here, and now part of the classroom. A primary agenda for each ethnic and social group is to learn how to move safely among various social groups and safely home again. They also wonder how to balance participation in other groups outside of their own community. These are issues about which they feel that African Americans have little to teach or model, because we can move nowhere safely or meaningfully.

This changing immigration and enculturation pattern has altered the expectations students bring to the classroom. These new challenges frustrate students, teachers, and administrators. A major cause of this frustration is the emerging confusion about what ought to be the purpose and goal of education. There is almost no agreement about how to integrate the needs of students (old and new), the academy (the larger enterprise of scholarship), the specific institution, and the larger society. This lack of consensus on even the most basic educational goals or priorities adds to the malaise gripping educational institutions. When students or faculty members wail out in exasperation about "political correctness," they are reflecting, although in a simpleminded way, the degree to which they do not know how to integrate the new cultural reality with any type of meaningful educational expectations. Black faculty have become for many, consciously and unconsciously, symbolic of this problem. This chapter will explore the dynamics of this shifting phenomenon and how the use of novels of resistance can be used to enhance the teaching process.

## USING NOVELS OF RESISTANCE

This chapter will discuss the use of novels of resistance as a method of teaching students to analyze complex cultural patterns and to develop greater intercultural empathy. By "novels of resistance" I mean primarily fictional works where the primary characters must struggle not only with emotional and interpersonal problems but also with their indigenous cultures. In these works the characters make a conscious decision to participate in their community but have self-consciously decided to challenge core cultural beliefs and values. In novels of resistance, it is clear that identity, family values, community, as well as suffering all flow in a complex and diverse cultural context. The primary characters are marginal not only by their choices but also by their social location. It is the contention of this chapter that novels can be more effective than case studies in understanding and appreciating the interplay of individuals, cultural values, and the process of healing and maturation. Novels of resistance can be effective in illustrating many of the cultural issues that students bring to the classroom. In these works the primary characters are part of and yet outside of their cultures, and as a result the relationship of personality to culture can be fully explored. In addition, given the insider-outsider status of many of the characters, the complexity, including the intergenerational quality and modernization of cultural patterns, can be examined in ways that students can transfer to other settings. Most important, the process of healing and accepting personal responsibility can be closely analyzed.

# LEARNING TO MOVE MEANINGFULLY
# BETWEEN MULTIPLE CULTURAL WORLDS

The United States may have begun as a "melting pot" (like many African Americans I resent this lie), but the nation is becoming even more diverse, and is less a "melting pot" than at any other time in its history. According to the U.S. Census Bureau, by the year 2050 nearly half the population of the United States will be composed of racial ethnic persons. Currently, 36 percent of all schoolchildren are people of color, and this group now constitutes 70 percent of all students in urban schools. The racial composition that exists in elementary and secondary schools will soon be reflected in postsecondary, graduate, and professional schools. This growing diversity of the United States has much deeper implications than that the United States is no longer primarily white/Anglo-Saxon and Protestant or that the country will simply be composed of individuals from a variety of different countries seeking to fit into American consumer culture. The most significant implication is that there may be at best few shared cultural values, no common worldview, and no agreed-upon national goals or commitments—all of which are important elements for any type of learning. More than ever before, an increasing number of individuals is coming to the educational enterprise with intense personal needs and a multiplicity of social agendas.

The growing "balkanization" of the United States can either be a cause for fear or an opportunity for a creative turning point in our nation's history. The only thing that is certain is that the new immigrants will not leave their heritage at the airport or the border crossing. They may have much to teach those who have lived in the United States longer and who are internal immigrants of one sort or another. We are witnessing growing numbers of foreign-language schools, Saturday morning cultural centers where children learn traditional custom and rituals, and communities that demand that schools, elections, and other public facilities be bilingual. This trend is also seen by the number of people who send their children to their home country to learn the native language and establish kinship ties. Growing numbers of immigrants plan to retire or spend part of the year in their home countries. The question facing new immigrants is precisely the issue that all U.S. residents have needed to resolve for the past three hundred years: the question of how to move meaningfully between multiple cultural worlds.

This growing complexity has contributed to many cities becoming more like mini-cities within larger metro complexes. For example, in 1992, when a jury acquitted four police officers accused in the videotaped beating of Rodney King and the people of Los Angeles rioted for six days, it became apparent that this is a city with over two hundred different cultural and ethnic groups with their own languages, arts, ideals, and in some cases different understanding of what it means to be a community. At times these various groups are at odds with their neighbors and with the city of Los Angeles itself. These communities asked and at times demanded that their native languages and customs be recognized. Even Asians, once called model immigrants for their desire to fit in with little disturbance, were now making demands on the rest of the culture. This new pattern forces questions never answered in the past about community, diversity, and how we treat those who are different. It is because of this that our nation continues to mishandle people, both here and abroad, who are different. Problems that we are unable to address in the classroom are also problems that are misjudged in other areas of life.

Educational paradigms need to respond to this changing cultural context in order to avoid old pitfalls and assumptions such as believing that teaching ought to transcend racial differences and assimilate people into the dominate culture, or educational theories that assume the existence of universal principles with which all students must be familiar. Nor can educational paradigms settle for simply teaching about exotic cultural differences. As educators we must develop paradigms that meet the needs of a racially and ethnically complex society. These new paradigms must confront a reality where an increasing number of students are people of color, while almost 80 percent of the teachers are white.[2] This statistic alone may suggest a clash of cultures and competing social agendas that require new approaches to teaching. It also means that as more teachers of color enter the classroom, both fellow teachers and students alike will grapple with and be confused by this changing reality. What is needed, as with each new generation, are new paradigms that integrate the demands of intellectual disciplines, the racial identity of students and teachers, and concepts of social change, power, and culture, if persons are to be educated for the changing future. Of paramount importance is the need for new paradigms that teach students how to analyze human behavior in relation to socially complex situations where there are competing social norms. In order to accomplish the last goal, students need the capacity to interpret various cultural patterns and to develop intercultural empathy.

## CLASSROOM REALITIES

I teach religion and psychology, which includes pastoral care and counseling, at Drew Theological Seminary. These courses integrate constructive theology, ethics, and clinical psychology. The goal is to introduce students to the practice of ministry with developmental and situational crises such as domestic violence, substance abuse, adolescent suicides, premarital counseling, and posttraumatic stress disorders. We not only explore the emotional aspects of these problems but also examine the spiritual collapse that often accompanies these conditions. I teach the required, introductory course, recommended for the second year of study for masters of divinity students. It is assumed that students have had other introductory courses in Bible, systematic theology, and church history and that they are in the process of taking field education, church at worship, ethics, and Christian education. The timing is important since pastoral care and several other courses taught during their middle years require that students begin to apply what they have learned in their more cognitively oriented classes.

The curriculum is dependent upon a student's ability to integrate cognitive with experiential learning. The student must be able to put theory into practice, and to critically reflect on their professional experiences. In short, they must be able to engage in praxis. Students need to know about the human condition, how we are created as social beings, and the implications of these ideas for developing structures that promote spiritual growth and healing. It is difficult for students to focus on these questions when they are actively afraid about their inability to move between and among competing communities.

The question, then, is how modern cultural diversity, balkanization, affects the processes of teaching and learning. Most teachers initially assume that a rich cultural and intellectual mix of students adds to the learning process and enriches the student's experience. Generally by midterm most teachers regret or lament the heterogeneous quality of their classrooms, feeling overwhelmed, frustrated, and lost. The challenge of attempting to achieve even modest educational goals makes some faculty feel the curse of Sisyphus might be a blessing by comparison. With conflicting norms and expectations, many students and teachers become frustrated and begin to question one another's role and function. Faculty feel that students are not as competent as they were in times past, and students question the authority and competence of faculty. Students are angry and distrustful of one another, and teachers are as contentious with one another as the students. It is possible that a significant aspect of what is functioning is that there is no center of gravity, that is, there is no agreement about what ought to be taught, for what purpose, or to what end. Several years ago a prestigious university was given a sizable grant to teach "the classics." That seems straightforward enough. After several years, the money had to be returned because there was no agreement among the faculty as to what constitutes "the classics." The more cynical among us might say that this is simply a classic example of political correctness, but the dilemma of this school may provide some insight as to what is happening in our educational environment.

What would it mean to have classic literature taught based on what was considered classical before 1930? What would it mean to have classic texts taught and not have any literary work from the Southern Hemisphere, Africa, or from women from any time period from any continent? Should deciding what is "classic" be a matter of what is widely known, skillfully written, or representative, containing a particular subject matter, relevance, or acclaim at the time it was written? More important, who should have input into this decision? These questions do not begin to broach the problem of what ought to be accomplished by teaching "classic texts." Is it assumed that learning "classic texts" will prepare students to engage in discussions with scholars worldwide who have their own "classic texts"? Or is it assumed that the most effective way of breaking out of an intellectual Tower of Babel is that there is a common language, "the classic text," of which all are familiar?

Every reasonable person would say that a little of both is desired, and this in moderation. It assumes a typically American approach to problems that assumes all major goals can be accomplished. This approach always leads to emptiness when one is eventually confronted with the realization that there is insufficient time and resources to accomplish all possible goals, at times conflicting, and that priorities need to be established. The most troubling questions are always, as in the Balkans, who makes decisions about participation, and how can an individual participate meaningfully?

I assume that consciously and unconsciously each student and faculty member brings this debate about "classic texts" to each and every class. They wonder if their education is intended to prepare them to take on a role in a "classical Western world," or to live in a diverse global community. The students appear to be unsure, and, more disturbing, they are uncertain about whether to trust my answers around these questions.

The question about "classic text" is always just below the surface and is reflected in most questions and responses in a number of subtle and obvious ways. As I teach racially diverse classes in pastoral care, I routinely focus on issues of family. In a class on marriage and family counseling where I present a lecture on marital conflict, invariably, a Korean student will give a short recitation on how conflicts are normally handled in Korean homes. This occurrence is typical in my class. At various times, students from Liberia, Ghana, India, Thailand, China, Mexico, or other countries may give similar short presentations about how men and woman fight in their homes. On initial observation, it is not clear whether these personal remarks are merely digressions, free associations, or attempts to make a personal connection to the presented material. There are times when students share their personal experience that it almost seems that they are challenging the authority of the teacher with the authority of their own culture. This does not always need to be done by students born outside of the United States. Students who self-identify as being from urban areas, Evangelical churches, a particular political ideology, sexual orientation, social class, age cohort, or geographic region—all may want to claim some exception to the principles of marital communications theory.

The cultural observations shared by the students may simply be instances where the students are attempting to bridge the cultural gap between the realities of their social norms and what they perceive to be the values presented in the class. But on observing how the students fail to integrate the theory in subsequent case studies, I suspect there may be a variety of other things happening. For instance, the student may be wondering whether the presented material has relevance for them and their community. They are wondering whether the approach of clinical psychology has any value outside of white, middle-class, American households. Another aspect of this "sharing" is their struggle with what will happen to their social role and location if they are perceived by their community to be using an approach that is nontraditional for their specific cultural group. This latter question always brings with it an uncertainty about how to understand their reference group, which is always going through a process of acculturation and social change. This is even more complex for immigrant communities where the community in the United States is similar to but different from the community back home and the student is undecided as to which community he or she may be functioning in at any given time. Many of the students are in a further quandary since they are unsure as to whether they will be functioning within their own ethnic group or whether they may be functioning in a community other than their own indigenous community. In short, the personal observations are the student's attempt, in part, to ask questions related to the interplay of culture and the intellectual material presented in class. And the teacher must know how to catch these pedagogical and cultural cues.

It is interesting that students are never very concerned about the simple truth or value of any theory or psychological approach to human problems. From the students' perspective, the issues of cultural and social relevance are more troubling than the technical merit of a psychological theory. The question they struggle with is the implication of the theory for their community and their place in that community when using Western ideals and concepts. Associated with this question is their struggle to decide in which community they might best use the theory effectively. The use of novels that address cultural conflicts allows students to explore questions about contradictory cultural realities and provides space to address a variety of other issues depending on the subject matter.

## WHO ARE THE STUDENTS IN SEMINARY?

A primary reason that students have difficulty analyzing complex cultural and social patterns is that they begin undergraduate and graduate education already overwhelmed by the realities of their life. In addition to struggling with intimidating social and cultural anxieties, there are numerous interpersonal problems they bring to the classroom. The majority of our students are between thirty and forty-five years of age. For the most part, they have already formed their professional identities in another field and are unsure how to transfer this knowledge to the practice of ministry. On one hand, they may attempt to simply apply previous problem-solving strategies to the tasks of ministry. Or, on the other hand, they may attempt to present themselves as a blank slate, with the expectation that seminary will give them everything they need to know about their new careers. For the most part, many of our students do not know what it means to be a student and to enter into a healthy, collaborative learning relationship.

Many of the students attending seminary are marginal individuals even within their own communities. Their marginality is not always the result of being part of a minority group, but they have still experienced strong feelings of social alienation for much of their lives. Typically this feeling of social alienation fosters a sense of being on the outside looking in, and then ambivalence about how to engage their community more effectively. It is not unusual that many are the adult children of alcoholics, had physical disabilities as children, or grew up in extreme poverty. With many seminary students feeling marginalized in their communities, novels of resistance reflect their experience of struggling with social and cultural demands. When individuals are acutely aware of their marginal status, they are quite sensitive to the demands placed on them by their culture and family, typically feeling humiliated or violated when they feel forced to comply with the expectations of others. The work of James Garbarino, Carl Bell, and others clearly indicates a deadening of mental agility when people feel stressed. Social alienation is a major stress. Being unable to interpret or know how to respond to the demands of culture or community would worsen this condition and increase the student's inability to think abstractly.

I am surprised by the number of students who seem to be unable to apply the concepts learned in the classroom, or integrate materials from multiple theoretical perspectives. When reading their papers, or their analyses of case studies, it appears as if most students have never had a course in the Bible, ethics, or theology. In fact, most students show little ability to use theory to gain additional insights in corporate or individual behavior. In addition to a cultural resistance to using theory as a hermeneutic to interpret experience, there are several factors that appear to interfere with the students' learning, their ability to think creatively, or their ability to allow me to help them with this process.

Typically, students enter seminary feeling a strong sense of dread about the multiple problems that will be confronting them in ministry. These problems at times include small and dying churches that need rejuvenation, issues of urban and rural communities in economic ruin, and public distrust of clergy because of a long history of clergy sexual abuse. Other concerns that seem to overwhelm students are the economic instability of many denominations and the lack of any meaningful vision by the leadership of their organization. Anticipating these problems tends to frighten students to the point where their cognitive abilities are reduced. The problems of their expectations for ministry are exacerbated by the large number of matriculating students who enroll in the master's degree program within two years of a major life crisis such as the death of a parent, divorce, medical illness, or unemployment. Typically the students spiritualize these problems with a belief that God was just trying to get their attention. It is almost impossible, from a teaching perspective, to have students imagine how they can care for someone in crisis when they are still in the midst of their own recovery. Living with crisis typically leads students to generate simplistic solutions to complex problems, and diminishes their ability to live with ambiguity or conflicting realities.

Because the students are more anxious, they bring their mild forms of balkanization into the classroom and approach their ethnic identity in a manner that increases the rigidity in their thinking. Typically, my students sit in three distinct groups: the Black students sit on my left, the Korean and Korean Americans sit toward the center and rear of the class, and whites sit on the right. Even while acknowledging an immense diversity within their cultural group, when confronted by another group, they work to assert their ethnic identity. This way of defining self provides clear categories to define others who are different, and thus limits the possibility for defining their own ethnic identity. The more anxious the students are, the more they assume various groups are distant from their own community.

## BLACK, MALE, AND TEACHING

All of the above issues—personal crisis, cultural and professional identities—are intensified for students by having a Black professor. My analysis is that my Blackness, my embodiment, makes them acknowledge feelings of powerlessness as they confront both the cultural, professional, and personal problems they are experiencing. This increased anxiety tends to inhibit their ability to think creatively and they feel overwhelmed by the learning process, to which they respond with frustration, guilt, and fear.

Despite several civil rights bills and social changes over the past fifty years, Blackness still represents suffering, chaos, and a lack of pride. These traits are experienced even more acutely when Blackness is encountered in males. I assume this is the case whether students are Black or non-Black. For Black students there is the feeling that I, a Black man, remind them of their second-class status. For all of the students there is the fear that I am unable to help them to prepare for the professional challenges that confront them. This is the case even when they enjoy the class—sadly, this enjoyment is more like professional or intellectual entertainment.

Of the many issues confronting me as a teacher, the most disquieting is the large numbers of Black, White, and Asian students who cannot identify with me as a model for how to approach the pastoral care aspects of ministry. If they cannot or will not use me as a model, then it is impossible for them to benefit from the skill, experience, and expertise I bring to the classroom. It is difficult for them to learn from someone who is seen as alien or who is thought to function in an environment in which they cannot imagine themselves practicing ministry. As I present material on how to interpret human behavior, or suggest counseling strategies, they are not able to see themselves engaging in the professional practice I outline since they think of me as existing in an alien environment. Many students—Black, White, Hispanic, and Asian—find it difficult to trust the expertise of Black faculty. Trusting in the knowledge or skills of Black faculty would require that they examine their presuppositions about ministry to the point where they also challenge their beliefs about how the world functions. Trust is related to having confidence that the person teaching them has the understanding of the subject matter to help them to be effective in their new career and can guide them through needed changes. It is hard for most persons to believe that an African American has the experience or expertise to help them negotiate this process. Last, at times they assume I will do the intellectual work for them. They expect that Blacks will use their time, space, and energy caring for their students' needs. Just as in the movies, I am the Black servant, since they are powerless to do the work for themselves. In the teaching environment, this means that we will think, plan, and integrate new materials for them, and they will just take this in by osmosis. My thesis is that they will do this in all classes, but this is more intense with people of color tending professional issues.

Despite the above problems, there may be a number of benefits to forcing students to have faculty whose embodiment makes them uncomfortable. Having a Black teacher increases the cultural reality and anxiety in class, and this matches the conflicts the students face in their communities. With the class experience matching their social life, though stressful, the students are more likely to transfer this learning to professional and social problems.

## A STRATEGY OF NOVELS

In response to the above problems, I have begun using novels in my courses. I use novels from Africa, the Middle East, and Russia, in addition to materials from the United States. Several novels I have found to be particularly useful are *Petals of Blood*[3] by Ngugi wa Thiong'o from Kenya; *Women at Point Zero*[4] by Nawal El Saadawi from Egypt; *Fathers and Sons*[5] by Ivan Turgenev from Russia; and *The Color of Water*[6] by James McBride and *Possessing the Secret of Joy*[7] by Alice Walker, both from the United States.

One novel that has been particularly useful has been Walker's *Possessing the Secret of Joy*. This story has a protagonist needing and seeking healing for a variety of conditions. She is grieving the death of a sister who died during a childhood ritual, and she has marital conflicts with an unfaithful husband in love with another woman. Tashi, the leading character, has an African American friend, Olivia, who is unable to show empathy for Tashi's choices or predicament. Tashi also struggles with the trauma of her own clitorectomy and has strong inner turmoil about how she fits into her culture. Her marginalization is due in part to being reared by parents who were influenced by African American missionaries. She is a woman at times caught between African cultural norms and Western cultural norms, traditional and modern. Tashi seeks healing in the United States with traditional psychiatrists and later journeys to Switzerland and meets with a Jungian who is sympatric but is unable to effect a cure. Throughout much of the book Tashi struggles with the need for self-discovery and for healing depression and trauma.

Not only is this text rich for the healing issues raised by the character Tashi, the cultural issues are even more complex and engaging. Tashi travels to the United States with her African American husband and lives there for a short time. She is from a country that has recently experienced a war of liberation and where the leaders of the liberation struggle are idealized and deified. There is the question for Tashi about what it means for her to fit into her culture, and at what cost. The decision to undergo the circumcision ritual is her attempt to belong by any means necessary. Most poignant in this novel is the collusion of the oppressor and the oppressed, although it is never entirely clear "who" the oppressor is. This is reflected in Tashi's mother's participation in Tashi's sister's ritual clitorectomy. This participation is an example of social violence toward women that benefits men, yet is performed by women. In this case, we see that one of the hands that held Tashi's sister down during the ritual, when she died, was that of her mother. Who is the oppressor in this story? The question of the oppressor is even more blurred when we recognize that all parties involved are both victim and victimizer.

There are other cultural elements in *Possessing the Secret of Joy* that make this book and others like it useful. The book is about an African ritual written by an African American. What does it mean to have individuals address cultural and social issues for another community or nation? The questions with all immigrant communities are: By whose values do they live? When do they live out each set of values? Alice Walker is African American, and therefore, the question of cultural imperialism is present. What does it mean for an African American to attempt to give voice for an African woman? Although the issue of female circumcision is not new and is addressed by both African women and men, it must be discussed within the context of this novel. This aspect of the book raises the question of gender imperialism and cultural imperialism. This issue is discussed in the book as Olivia, Tashi's best friend, works hard to convince Tashi not to have the circumcision. The relationship of African American to African culture emerges throughout the text, as well as whether there can be universal values of care and concern that can be applied to any circumstance. Last, there is the question about where and how Tashi finds her healing. In the novel Tashi finds healing as she asserts control over her life and in the process kills the woman who had performed her circumcision. It is difficult to say in this story what constitutes healing for this individual who had suffered so much loss. In most novels of resistance it is always difficult to state with any certainty how to define the healing process. This ambiguous quality is in part what makes these texts so interesting.

To use novels in the classroom I have found that I had to teach students how to read a text. The problem of learning how to read a text requires the use of theory, personal effect, and judgment. The dynamics of this process are the same whether students are reading a novel or listening to parishioners discuss problems in their lives. In pastoral care, this reading requires that they imagine themselves in a professional role making critical use of their personal histories. Even more important, when I begin the class with a work from Ghana or Kenya, the students have a non-threatening way to confront the reality of my race. It is a means of introducing the racial dimensions of the class and of the teacher. When asked to discuss how the issue of race is related to issues in the class, or in U.S. society in general, Black students discuss their rage about problems in the United States, and whites become apologetic or defensive. Instead, when we begin with a novel outside of the U.S. context, students are more likely to use theory to analyze what is taking place. If they can learn to identify with a person of color in the text, it may allow them to identify with me and my Blackness.

## QUESTIONS TO PROCESS STUDENT REFLECTION

There are several questions that I process with the students as we discuss each novel. The first two questions come from the field of anthropology and are related to the use of universal, relative, and evolutionary methods of evaluating human behavior. The students are forced to consider multiple and conflicting cultural viewpoints, both between people and within individuals. In the book *Petals of Blood*, the students are observing four different characters adjusting to life after a revolution. The lead character of the book *Fathers and Sons* might be viewed as a hero, as immature, or as emotionally disturbed depending on the point of view one uses to understand his behavior. It is essential that the students do not privilege any value system over another. The students need to appreciate the variety of ways by which people can respond in healthy and unhealthy ways.[8] Since these various strategies are frequently in conflict, their understanding for the need to live with ambiguity and dissonance will clearly be deepened.

The next question from the field of anthropology and cross-cultural studies asks students to consider whether persons are being evaluated from an "emic" or an "etic" perspective. David Augsburger discusses the importance of being able to describe another person in categories that would make sense to that person. He describes this as transspection. Transspection means to essentially join another in their world and to describe their actions from their perspective. Are students able to discuss the choices of McBride's mother from her history as a Jewish woman living in Harlem and passing for Black?[9]

The next question comes from psychoanalytic theory. In the field of psychoanalysis, an interesting concept is the notion of secondary gain. This is related to the idea of homeostasis, which assumes that the problems and concerns of a social system may also provide some of the balance that holds a system together. Or, put another way, people cannot easily separate themselves from even a destructive community if that culture also provides for them essential connection to the universe or gives them structures of meaning. Even though Tashi is aware that her participation in the female circumcision rite will be harmful, she chooses to participate because her tribe provides the only structure of meaning for her life. This insight is supported by the work of Frantz Fanon, who makes us aware of the interdependence of social systems.[10]

The next issue for students is to analyze systematically the process of change. Frequently, clergy do not know how to facilitate change, either within individuals or in groups. Much like the notion of salvation, or love, this does not take place at one moment and with one act. In discussing the novels, the students are required to discuss the process of change using multiple places in the stories, different types of behavior, and different types of indicators of this change. Margaret Kornfeld, in her book *Cultivating Wholeness*,[11] presents excellent examples of how to understand the process of change in individuals and in groups. Frantz Fanon in *Black Skin, White Masks*[12]; William Cross and his work on Cultural Identity Theory[13]; Ronald Carter in *The Influence of Race and Racial Identity in Psychotherapy*[14]; and Beverly Tatum in *Why Are All the Black Kids Sitting Together in the Cafeteria?*[15] are great resources in understanding how individuals grapple with their racial and ethnic identities in the process of this change.

With these interdisciplinary questions, it is hoped that students begin to develop the capacity for empathy. Empathy is the ability to think and feel about a situation in a similar way that another person might feel and think about that experience—it is to see, think, and feel as if one person were the other, then to think and feel about the situations using one's own social, cultural, racial, and gender identity. This "back and forth" viewing of the world through the eyes and skin of another requires an act of imagination and creativity. Empathy uncovers an inherent connectedness, that is, a universal self-awareness that comes into corporate consciousness and that reflects our interdependence with others. We acknowledge our membership as part of more immediate communities, but this does not pull us away from participation in a wider social reality. It is in the interplay of participation in a smaller, cultural, ethnic community, as well as our membership in wider human communities, that true creativity is born, and that needs to happen for learning to take place.

The processing of these questions begins to facilitate students becoming more aware of the dynamics of their own culture, and to consider what it means to experience the culture of others. It also begins a process of enabling them to appreciate psychological theories within this complex cultural matrix, and to imagine how this may impact another. Most important, it forces an integration of all the wisdom they have accumulated, in other classes, from parents, their communities, and other cultures in attempting to address human suffering.

# THREE

# E-Racing While Black

## Stephen G. Ray Jr.

*How do educators understand the idea of the "racialized imagination" and its relationship to theological education? What particular challenges do Black theological educators face in trying to teach past this imagination, in other words to e-race the faith? What pedagogical practices are available to accomplish the work of e-racing teaching about the Christian faith?*

## THE TEACHING CHALLENGE

A challenge that faces theological educators today is that of inclusion—the creation of an inclusive learning environment and the inclusion of hitherto marginalized voices in the Christian tradition. These two acts of pedagogy are, by my estimation, projects that counter the history of what Carter G. Woodson referred to as "mid-education," which characterizes much of the educational process in the North American context. Theological education in the United States, and elsewhere I suspect, has been, and to a great extent remains, a captive of what I term the "racialized imagination" of modernity. By this term, I mean to identify the general tendency in modernity, and in the specific history of the United States, to interpret human reality—reflectively, contemporaneously, and proleptically—as the story of various and differing racial groups. An enduring legacy of the system of chattel slavery in the context of the United States has been the total racialization of the American imagination. There is no aspect of contemporary thinking or historical reflection that escapes this tinting. Substantial work done in various fields has demonstrated that this racialization of humanity and our history function primarily to sustain and recapitulate the workings of the regime of white supremacy by coloring, or some might say discoloring, all of the normative institutions of Western history and culture "white." This whitening of history has been particularly pronounced in relation to the Christian tradition and the teaching of it in schools of religion and theological education. It is this teaching of the Christian tradition as a captive of the "racialized imagination" that I term mis-education.

I believe that this pervasive pedagogical reality is mis-education because it relies on a distorted interpretation of human reality and history. Issues generic to time (i.e., the particular history of geographically and culturally distinct Christian communities) are distorted in such a way that curiosity is diminished and students immediately experience a racial turfdom in relation to a history (or histories) that they may know little or nothing about. So, frequently our Black students come away from engagements with church history and various theological traditions with a feeling that their experience is neither present nor relevant, and our white students come away with an ambiguously diachronic sense of ownership and alienation that leads to the experience of their learning of Christian history as being contrived. This situation arises, of course, from one of the great tragedies of American church history, which has been the appropriation of the entire Christian tradition by the regime of white supremacy. By this I mean that it is too often the case that the "mainstream" Christian tradition is rendered as an ethnic and racial legacy claimable only by those who share a particular identity. "Others," and their ecclesial traditions, are often treated as quaint interpretations of the tradition but rarely the embodiment of it. In my teaching, my philosophy and method are focused largely on attempting to counter this mis-education by introducing the idea and inculcating the sensibility that the Christian tradition belongs to *all of us*.

## MIS-EDUCATION AT WORK

A situation that frequently arises in my first-year class on theology and church history is that African American students are somewhat ambivalent about the texts we read that emerge from the tradition until we reach the texts having to do with the Black church; and conversely, white students feel a historical claim on these texts of the tradition *until* we reach the texts about the Black church. To the outside observer it might seem as if we were dealing with ecclesial realities as disparate as the Ethiopian Coptic Church and the Appalachian Holiness movement. But, of course, we are not. Anyone familiar with American church history knows that the differences between "Black churches" and "white churches," particularly of the Evangelical brand, in terms of hymnody, theological outlook, and piety are in shades and not absolute monochromes. Certainly, there are unique developments in varying communities (e.g., spiritual vs. counterpointal hymns), yet these have more to do with specific experience and tradition (e.g., Methodist as opposed to Congregationalist) than with stark ecclesial differences. Yet, this gap in understandings of "ownership" exists and has consequence for our students. Two examples will make this point.

I was given a paper by an African American student who took John Calvin to task for the reformer's doctrine of predestination. The paper itself was well written and well argued. The problem was with the substance of the student's reading of Calvin. The student critiqued Calvin on the point that his "black and white" (the student's words, not mine) view of who was the recipient of God's grace and election and who was not was an explicit authorization for oppression and had no place in the preaching of the gospel of love. In her estimation, Calvin was little different than the long line of "false teachers" who had branded Blacks as those outside of God's providential grace. While it is true that many have critiqued Calvin on the tension between election and love present in his doctrine of predestination, this student's critique turned not on this tension, but rather on her reading the presumptive equivalence between whiteness and election in the racialized American imagination into Calvin's text. The situation is complexified even more by a conversation I had previously had with this student. We were talking about someone we both knew who had recently died in her forties. We both bemoaned a life too short. Toward the end of the conversation the student intoned words I had heard many times growing up: "Well, it's a tragedy, but when your number is up . . ." Here was a student who clearly operated with a theological framework informed by Calvin, yet felt such alienation toward the person that no affinity could be seen. Was the student simply naive? I think not.

My assessment of the situation was/is that this particular student was reading Calvin as a "white guy" talking about election and the preferred recipients of God's grace, in a context in which these were synonymous with whiteness. So, even though she was reading someone who had been particularly influential on her theological worldview (i.e., Providence), all she could see was another text in a long line that legitimated and divinely sanctioned the status and final destiny of white people vis-à-vis Black people. Clearly, she felt ownership neither of nor by the tradition that Calvin represented. In my estimation, the student's worldview was largely conditioned by the way she had learned and experienced *which* Christian tradition she was a part of, and which she was not a part of.

Let us be clear about the extent of loss here. Clearly, the student's alienation from the broad tradition of Christianity was such that many of its resources and much of its wisdom was unavailable to her in meaningful ways. The mirror of this student's loss was/is that the wisdom and witness of her "tradition" is largely lost to the broad tradition of the faith. This is particularly troubling given that the basis of the alienation going on here is the earlier mentioned captivity of the tradition by a regime of knowledge that upholds social relations that are deeply problematic, if not downright sinful.

Fast forward to an example of how we can concretely see the loss this alienation brings to the tradition. The example is drawn from a sermon that I preached a few years back in the Marquand Chapel at Yale Divinity School, on the occasion of Martin Luther King Jr.'s birthday. I preached about Nat Turner as an important link in the line of witnesses that stretched from Elijah to King, both of whom had been raised up by God to strike at the root of sinful and unjust social systems that were destroying the bodies and spirits of God's children. The sermon was framed in a way to contend that this was a line of witnesses to which we were all heirs, and from which we could all draw strength. After the sermon, a faculty member emeritus came up to me and said he had never thought of himself as an heir of faith to Turner, even though he had spent much of his life combating the evil of racism with his words and his body. While he questioned the methods of Turner, he likewise questioned the methods of Elijah, but had always considered himself an heir to the latter. Need I say that the faculty member was Euro-American? Would he have felt differently if I had used John Brown, or, say, Dietrich Bonhoeffer, as my example? Or would he have felt the same dissonance if I had presumptively classed him and all the other "whites" in the congregation with those against whom God had raised Turner in judgment? Here is, I believe, another case of a person of faith claiming, and being claimed by, a tradition predicated on the racialized American imagination.

With the preceding examples I hope to have illustrated the way that the racialized imagination can affect the way that persons orient themselves to the Christian tradition and some ways that we are all diminished by the situation. Let me make explicit a working assumption that underlies this piece: Whether one is teaching in a seminary or a divinity school, the work of a teacher of theology is not primarily to acquaint students with an archaic or exotic religious tradition but rather to help them connect to a living tradition of which they are a part and from which they can draw life and inspiration. If one works with this as a guiding principle, it is clearly problematic when students enter our classrooms with a truncated theological imagination that unnecessarily cuts them off from imbibing from the full breadth of the Christian tradition.

Allow me to continue this discussion by identifying several challenges that I experience in my pedagogical practice as I engage in what I call e-racing the faith—by which I mean demystifying the idea of race and contesting its grip on the religious imagination. I will follow these ruminations with some strategies, or better interventions, that I employ to further this work of e-racing.

## THE CHALLENGE OF EMBODIMENT

The first challenge that I would identify is directly related to the issue of embodiment. I am Black. As a Black person pedagogically e-racing the faith, I find that there is a certain type of reasoning that students immediately fall into when the subject turns to race. Specifically, they encounter discussions about the faith and *race* as being primarily about *racism* and the faith. While not unrelated, the two issues are not the same. Though it is true that the idea of race is the necessary predicate of racism by the former (race) maintaining the condition of the possibility for the latter (racism) to express itself, I think there is more than a noetic difference between the two. Race is, as Anthony Apiah puts it, an ideational theory of difference that relies for its meaning on a complex of ideas and significations. This web of ideas then forms the prism through which racialized bodies are seen.[1] Racism is then the material enactments that emerge from these perceptions and ideas.

Three of the dimensions of this complex that bear most immediately on the teaching enterprise are: (1) the belief in the ontological irreducibility of racialized bodies—the assumption that
what is most real about human persons can be derived from a
proper racial categorization of their bodies, (2) the assumption
that bodies racialized as Black cannot generally engage in a mul-
tivalent, textured conversation about matters of race but rather
engage in these discussions as a single-issue discourse, and (3) the
interpretation of subjectivity and objectivity as nonracial categories with the consequence that racialized bodies are incapable of
"objective" reflections on race in the same way nonracial bodies
are. These assumptions manifest themselves in several ways, perhaps the most important for this discussion being the not infre-
quent assumption made by my white students that I am
self-interested in the conversation in a way that they are not. This
assumption is most often couched in questions about what this
conversation has to do with learning to do ministry in "their context." Most are simply oblivious[2] to the fact that their presumptions about the faith have everything to do with their "interest" in
the conversation.

A consequence to teaching as well as the relational dynamics in
the academcy is that any discussion about race by a Black body is
presumptively reduced to a discussion about racism more generally,
and my experience of it specifically. *Ism* is then the primary suffix
heard when the letters *r-a-c* are spoken, particularly by Black bodies.
A consequence of this is that "white" embodiment is allowed to
remain invisible. Put another way, white people in the discussion
have little way of making sense of themselves in these discussions
apart from how they are being unfairly "implicated" in discussions of
racism. These discussions are experienced then as assault.[3] As might
be expected, for my white students all of the defense mechanisms
kick in, including personal guilt and resentment when I as a Black
body talk about race. For my Black students, there is frequently the
satisfaction of naming the heresy of the racialization of the faith but

not a sense of themselves as players as race is performed in our context. In both cases, the problematic assumption remains—that race is an appropriate category to utilize in delineating the particulars of the Christian tradition. In recognizing this first challenge, I am placing the issue of embodiment at the fore of any pedagogical considerations for those concerned with the project of e-racing the tradition. While the texture of the significance of embodiment will bear the nuances of context, it is vitally important to see that whether the practitioner is Black, white, or some other hue, that person's embodiment will affect the classroom dynamics when the discussion is about race. Bearing notice of this reality, and what it may mean in a given context, is essential to the project.

The second challenge that I face is the reality that most of my students come unprepared to this discussion about the ideological appropriation of the Christian tradition by the racialized imagination. That is to say, like most North Americans, the belief in the ontological reality of race, and its ensuing implications, is as immediate to my students as the air that they breathe. As well, many of them come from social and ecclesial contexts in which the only encounter that they have had with discourses and intellectual projects that challenge the racial hegemony of the American imagination and the culture it creates has been in the midst of the culture wars raging since the 1970s.[4] Consequently, many of my students will experience this intervention as an act of "political correctness" if it is done in a ham-fisted or strident fashion.

The first two points lead to a third challenge, namely, creating a pedagogical and theological space in which we can engage in what I term a "loving exorcism." By this I mean that the creation of a nonthreatening discursive space in which the presumptive racial character of the Christian tradition can be named and the system that gives the presumption currency challenged. By problematizing racialized historical vision for my students, I hope to begin the work of challenging their preconceived notions of ownership of the Christian tradition and to create a ground upon which education is possible in a racialized context. A ground upon which the wisdom of figures as disparate as Augustine, Aquinas, Julian of Norwich, Turner, King, and Tillich is available to us all.

In spite of these challenges, I believe it is entirely possible for us to recognize this problematic situation and to engage in small acts that reclaim the Christian tradition from this racialized imagination with the faith such that the cumulative effect will be the creation of a learning environment in which our students can be nourished from the deep wells of the Christian tradition. To wit, I offer two interventions that I use in my classroom.

## NAMING OUR ANCESTORS

There are several ways that we can engage the racialized assumptions that many of our students will have about the Christian tradition. We can, as one of my colleagues in an introductory theology and history class does, emphasize the fact that a significant number of the early church fathers were African. This is an important and necessary intervention, but it is only a beginning. It is a necessary, yet provisional, beginning because our students do not come to us as tabula rasa, namely, with a racialized understanding of the entirety of human history. We must be clear that a working assumption of many in our culture is that although Carthage, Egypt, and so forth may be in Africa, these places, and their inhabitants, are *not* like the rest of Africa: namely, Black. In his book, *The Disuniting of America*, Arthur Schlesinger gives voice to this understanding of history and identity:

> Any relationship between Egyptians, whatever color they may have been, and black Americans is exceedingly tenuous. . . . Black Americans do not trace their roots to Egypt. The great majority of their ancestors came from West Africa, especially the Guinea coast. They were from a variety of tribes and spoke a variety of languages; Professor Ali Mazrui tells us that Africa contains some distinct ethnic and linguistic groups. Any homogeneity among slaves

derived not from the African tribe but from the American plantation.[5]

Beyond an exemplification of the presumed absence of any connection between living African American communities and the great ancient societies from which the church emerged, Schlesinger's observation also identifies another pervasive feature of the racialized American imagination: namely, that most, if not all, attempts to construct a connection between African Americans and any culture other than that evolved during slavery is little more than ideological speculation. The pervasiveness of this assumption is evident in the Black Athena debate still raging in parts of the academy.[6] The effect of this presumption is that when biographical texts properly note that theologians such as Augustine were of Latin lineage, many of our students then conceive of him as somewhat of an early colonial. As we know, colonials in Africa are almost exclusively conjured by images of whites.

If a strategy of emphasizing the African origins of the church is only a beginning, how might we continue this work of redemption? It is important to recognize that the intuition of the approach just outlined is correct—we must begin our intervention in our earliest readings from and about the Christian tradition. We must, however, recognize that as with any other system of bondage, it is necessary to name both the subject of captivity and the forces that seek its enslavement. In the case before us, this means that we have to name the racialization of the Christian tradition and the project to which it is in service—the imaginative maintenance of white privilege in the American context.

My current approach to this necessary intervention has two moments. First, it takes seriously the need to begin with texts to which the students feel some organic connection; and second, it begins this intervention immediately. In the context in which I taught during the preparation of this piece, a seminary in the Reformed tradition, this meant I usually began with the writings of Augustine. I have some confidence that when students read the *Confessions* or *City of God* they will have heard these ideas before, either through explicit attribution or simply by echoes of the tradition heard in sermons or through Christian education materials. Additionally, by taking advantage of this organic connection, I hope to also tap into the presumptive authority of the Augustinian tradition. The earlier I can get students to explore a new imaginative landscape in which it is not theological commitment but rather race that is the source of connection to the tradition, the more likely they will be to develop these sensibilities toward the tradition and apply them to figures closer in time and cultural proximity to us (i.e., Luther and Calvin).

The second characteristic of my approach takes seriously, as earlier noted, the reality that most of my students come unprepared to this discussion about the ideological appropriation of the Christian tradition by the racialized imagination. That is to say, like most North Americans, the belief in the ontological reality of race, and its ensuing implications, is as the primary sense-making category available to my students when they consider issues germane to African American and Euro-American histories. A corollary is that most students, Black and white, approach discourse about race as necessarily oppositional, with the appropriate categories of meaning being resentment and guilt. Here I draw on the insight of Beverly Daniel Tatum in her article "Talking about Race, Learning about Racism: The Application of Racial Identity Development Theory in the Classroom," in which she observes:

> The introduction of these issues of oppression often generates powerful emotional responses in students that range from guilt and shame to anger and despair. If not addressed, these emotional responses can result in student resistance to oppression related content areas. Such resistance can ultimately interfere with the cognitive understanding and mastery of the material.[7]

Having this as a backdrop, my initial intervention may seem a bit simple. I usually begin by saying at some appropriate time in our small-group section conversation: "Augustine wasn't a white guy, nor, for that matter, was he a Black guy." I then go on to clarify the point that I am making: namely, that what we intend by these terms—racial identification—would have made no sense to Augustine at all as he thought about himself. I then briefly talk about how these are identities that have been constructed over the last three hundred to four hundred years and should not be retrojected back into history. This intervention usually takes all of five minutes, but it accomplishes several purposes.

By problematizing racialized historical vision, up front, for all of my students, I hope to begin the work of challenging their preconceived notions of ownership of the Christian tradition. I also hope to lay the groundwork to make a similar claim when we come to other figures in the tradition (e.g., Aquinas, Julian of Norwich, Martin Luther, etc.). With these later figures I make the same point in a different way. I delineate the historical reality of being an inhabitant of Europe and the ideological reality of having an identity signified by the idea of whiteness. As with Augustine, I will say something like, "Calvin wasn't a white guy. . . . If you called him one to his face he probably wouldn't know what you were talking about." Certainly, I make note, "white people," as such, are generally of European heritage, but I also note that to then say that all people who have ever lived on the land mass we identify as Europe were white does not follow. My warrant for making this move is that the same specificity that we, as teachers, apply to other matters of historical identity and self-understanding must also be applied to ideas of race. How many of us would, in good conscience, consistently refer to the pre-Columbian indigenous peoples of the Eastern Seaboard of what is today the United States as North Carolinians?

There are two purposes that this approach seeks to accomplish. First, I am implicitly attempting to objectify and externalize racial identity for the *entire* class. This allows the creation of a discursive environment in which we are not talking about the members of the class, but rather about the intervention of ideas in history. In my estimation this goes a long way to meeting the problem outlined earlier by Tatum. As well, this approach reinforces the need for students to appreciate the generally helpful tendency of being fully attentive to the specificity of the Christian tradition.

In my engagement with issues surrounding the appropriation of the Christian tradition by the racialized American imagination I never lose sight of the fact that I am *not* teaching a class on racial hegemony and identity formation. I am participating in the teaching of a class on the Christian tradition, its history, and theology. The appropriation of the Christian tradition by the racialized American imagination is not, therefore, the topic of conversation. Rather, its consideration is done in the service of making the tradition, which is the topic of conversation, accessible to *all* of my students. This project of inclusion is not solely a discursive undertaking. It is necessary, as well, to be attentive to issues of course design and the selection of materials. The selection and presentation of texts from the Christian tradition, both primary and secondary, play a role in the work of liberating the tradition from its racial captivity. Again, I offer a small intervention that may be a part of this work.

## TEXTUAL MEDIATION

The texts our students read are perhaps the enduring legacy that we give them in our introductory classes. For better or worse, the texts they engage will, for many students, be their conversation partners throughout their ministry. Their sense of what ideas are important to the Christian tradition, and who are the significant commentators in that tradition, will be formed largely by those they encounter during their time with us. It is therefore important that we take seriously this project of inclusion as we design our courses and reading lists.

In the classes that I took at divinity school, and in the courses that I have taught thus far in my career, the voices of marginalized communities have functioned largely as critics of the tradition. Whether they be the works of early Christian mothers, or contemporary feminists, liberationists, or Black theologians, it is often the case that they are positioned in the conversation so as to bring critiques of the already examined works of male European or Euro-American theologians. So, Judith Plaskow or Valerie Saiving are read to critique Niebuhr,[8] Gustavo Gutiérrez is brought in to critique the materialist culture of modernity in general and the Roman Catholic tradition in particular,[9] James Cone is counted upon to unleash the withering flames of righteous fury against the "white" American theological tradition,[10] and Hildegard De Bingen is read as a counterfoil and more "human" alternative to Anselm's approach to the atonement. While these are certainly important, and necessary, critiques, it is important to note both how they are used in class, and what this usage signifies to our students about the place in the Christian tradition of these texts and the communities from which they emerge.

By placing the texts of historically marginalized communities at the "margins" of the conversation, we communicate several messages to our students. The primary message is, of course, that at the legitimate core of the Christian tradition are the works that are the subject of these critiques. So, these normative voices may be seen as needing correction, but their normativity is not called into question. A supplementary, yet still powerful, message that we communicate is that the genius of these works, and the communities from which they emerge, is found in their role as criticism. Implicit in this message is an agnosticism about the capacity of these originating communities to produce works that are generally constructive to the Christian tradition. Many of our students experience these thinkers as primarily kibitzers and only vaguely as primary contributors to the tradition.

Another implication of the customary placement of texts, which bears directly on the subject of this essay, is the gap between the voice that is given to the African American theological tradition and the faith experience of our African American students. As noted by theologians such as Cecil Cone and J. Deotis Roberts, works such as *God of the Oppressed*[11] serve to illuminate the voice of criticism within the African American theological tradition but do little to express the constructive genius of the tradition.[12] Additionally, because of the strident character of works such as *God of the Oppressed*, our conversations about the text often stumble on the type of alienation earlier noted by Tatum.[13] We thus have a situation in which African American students may feel only liminal inclusion, and Euro-American students may be confirmed in the general, social common sense that the major cultural and religious tender that African Americans bring to the discussion is derivative anger. This is not the type of environment planned, or hoped for, by most theological educators. How then might we use texts in ways that illumine for *all* of our students their place in the Christian tradition? Here again, I will offer small interventions—the first about selection and the second about presentation—that can go some way to accomplish this project of inclusion.

Before outlining an approach to text selection, let me first take on a major concern that looms large in this conversation: namely, the appropriate recognition of influential voices in the tradition. It is and ever will be the case that because the historical trajectory of the Christian faith has winded through first the Roman and later other European empires, a predominance of writings conserved by the tradition has been male and European, either ancient or contemporary. This is simply historical fact. What we make of this historical texture, however, is entirely up to the current generation of teachers. This is made clear by the thorough ignorance of many teachers of theology, myself included, of the Coptic tradition of Christianity, which has far more antiquity than either the Roman, Protestant, or Evangelical traditions of the West. So, while it is a responsible act of pedagogy to maintain the tradition, and, one hopes, to contribute to it, it is entirely up to us how we will accomplish this preservation. An appropriate place to begin is to ask why we are engaged in this preservation in the first place.

I suspect, as earlier noted, that many teachers of theology are concerned to engage the tradition in a way that nourishes the contemporary generation of church theologians—our students. If a significant part of this process is formation, we must take seriously that a part of this formation is teaching our students to orient themselves to the tradition in a way that does not unreflectively replicate their racialized misorientation to human history. Given that much of the contemporary canon, and its appropriation of the texts of the Christian tradition, has been formed by an often implicit, sometimes explicit, commitment to the reiteration of the racialized Western (here, read white) tradition that has been a founding ideological underpinning of the racial imperialism of the last several centuries, it seems the task before those concerned with this misappropriation must take seriously a new approach to canon formation and use. Here I offer a provocation. Treat each use of texts from the tradition in the development of a course as an invitation to the formation of a provisional canon appropriate to the needs of the church in our context.

As I hope to have made clear, e-racing the faith is a paramount need for the contemporary church. Let me be clear: I am not suggesting that we do away with the teaching of significant texts within the tradition, like some colleagues in more Evangelical contexts have done, or treat them as ephemera as happens in some more progressive contexts. Rather, I am suggesting that we take seriously the fact that our presentation of these texts participates in their work of formation, either as a reinforcement of untoward interpretations or in retrievals more faithful to our project in the first place.

There are three textures of the transmission of tradition that I suggest we ought to be attentive to in taking a constructive approach to provisional canon formation. These nuances are weight, aesthetics, and dialogue. As to the first, I believe we must take seriously both the literal and figurative weight that we impute to the texts that we assign. The average first-year student will assume that a book that is purchased is more important than an article that is distributed. This assumption is rooted in the unspoken message that the book is worthy of their investment. Otherwise, why would we ask them to purchase it in these times of high tuition and decreased financial aid? Although it may simply be an observance of copyright law on our part, most of our students do not have the legal sophistication to make this connection. Consequently, they will initially assign more intellectual weight to the readings that materially weigh more. So, as we "weigh" the books we will use, it is vitally important we not relegate the texts that assist in the work of e-racing to course packets and require that our students purchase tomes that reiterate the very presumptions about the faith that we are trying to contest.

A way that we can take weight seriously is by first assessing what it is that we are trying to accomplish with a particular text. Are we prescribing texts as an introduction for theological students whom we presume are going to do further work in our discipline? Or are we preparing graduate students for comprehensive exams and cultivating a literacy in the broad-range texts that will be necessary for their craft? If we are, as this chapter is concerned with, framing for our first-year students a way of interpreting the tradition, then we can and should give weight as is appropriate to the task, and not as many of us mislearned it: namely, in a way that privileges the androcentric/Eurocentric voice. So, it is entirely possible to put Reinhold Niebuhr, Paul Tillich, and others on reserve or in a course packet and to require the purchase of constructive texts that construe the tradition through a richer multiplicity of voices. Or, we can make sure that any texts we prescribe for purchase have as a guiding principle this nuanced approach to the tradition.

This approach still leaves open the question of what to do with texts such as those of Augustine, Calvin, and other formative voices of the Western tradition. As I hope to have suggested in the previous section, uses of these texts are important occasions to do the work of e-racing the faith. So, works such the *Confessions* and the *Institutes*[14] ought to be prescribed, but with provisos that they should be treated as significant work done by Christian theologians who demonstrably were *not* white guys.

Aesthetics in text selection is significantly important because the covers and illustrations that a given text uses may so forcefully reiterate the very whitening of the tradition that we are trying to contest, which confounds the work of e-racing the faith, no matter how forceful the interventions we engage in otherwise. An example is in order. On the cover of the particular edition of Augustine's *Confessions*[15] that we used in an introductory history and theology class was a medieval painting of Augustine decked in finery contemporary to the artist. The centuries dividing the creation of the painting and Augustine mean that this could not possibly have been a picture of Augustine but was rather an expression of the sensibility and piety of the painter. Here I use the language of "picture" quite intentionally because we sometimes need to remind ourselves that we live in the photographic age. By this I mean that we live in an age in which there is some presumptive connection between the rendering of a subject and the subject itself. The idea of iconic and interpretive portraiture is not as immediate to members of our classes as it may have been to generations gone by. This is particularly the case when the presumptive connection of rendering and subject are race. Put plainly, if our students', and our own, presumptions about the tradition are, as I have suggested, racialized, then what is reinforced most powerfully, even if only subliminally, is that Augustine was a white guy. As many social scientists have demonstrated, images overpower speech. So, no matter that we would wish otherwise, the covers and illustrations of the texts we use either do the work of contesting the racial captivity of the tradition, or they further its bondage. What I am contending, therefore, is that to the extent possible we must either use racially neutral, or when left no alternative—if say a particular text is with all its problems the best translation available—we must problematize the presumptive connections that our students make as we present the text.

Finally, the way that we bring various texts into dialogue with one another in our classes is significantly important. For the first few years that I taught, when I approached the issue of sin as a category of theological anthropology, I would begin with Reinhold Niebuhr's *Nature and Destiny of Man*,[16] followed closely by reading Martin Luther King Jr.'s *Letter from Birmingham Jail*.[17] I came to realize that not only was I privileging Niebuhr's text but I was also privileging his voice as the Christian account of sin and theological anthropology. So, even though *Letter* and other texts were used to problematize his Eurocentric/androcentric approach (i.e., Elizabeth Johnson's *She Who Is*[18]), Niebuhr remained the voice of the tradition. If indeed, the critiques embedded within the use of these other texts were correct, and Niebuhr's vantage point was in many ways a distortion of the dogma upon which the tradition was founded, then why should his be the dominant voice?

I subsequently structured the reading to begin with a full reading of Howard Thurman's *Jesus and the Disinherited*.[19] As any reader of the text knows, Thurman makes some points that are very similar to Niebuhr's, but the difference is, of course, that the spokesman for the tradition destabilizes the presumptive identity of the tradition. By beginning with Thurman we are engaging the perennial issues of theological anthropology (i.e., sin and redemption) as they were framed by mid-twentieth-century North American discourses, but in such a way that we are immediately problematizing the workings of racial oppression in our very construction of what it means to understand being human. By allowing Thurman to set the terms of the dialogue, the class participants are immediately able to experience several textures within their engagement with the tradition. Most significantly, they are able to hear the tradition in a voice inflected by the African American experience. This experience can close the gap that is opened between my students because of the faulty presumptions many of them bring to the classroom. So, the Black and other students of color are able to "read" themselves as interpreters of the tradition in a way often unavailable to them. As well, my white students are able to experience a texture of the tradition that destabilizes their notions of racialized ownership, yet they also experience an account very familiar to them because it is in an idiom very familiar to them: late modern Protestant. By rearranging the way the texts are brought into dialogue, we are then able to accomplish two of the significant goals laid out in the beginning of the chapter: open the tradition for our Black students and recenter the way our white students orient themselves to the tradition away from a racialized appropriation.

## CONCLUSION

I began this chapter by problematizing what I believe is a central issue that faces teachers of theology who are concerned with creating an inclusive learning space and, additionally, cultivating a connection between their students and the great tradition that is the Christian faith. What I hope to have suggested is that the "racialization" of faith and tradition creates a seductive yet finally destructive ground for mis-education. A point that I have only intimated, but that is nonetheless critical in our assessment of the situation, is that the continued racialization of the faith contributes to not only the reiteration of the ideational structures that undergird systems of racial oppression but also ensures their transmission to future generations. If racism is sin, as many, but sadly not all, North American Christian communities believe, then the willful participation in its continued infection of faith is an act of apostasy. I use this language not merely for rhetorical effect but rather to bring attention to the critical need to take seriously the work of *e-racing* the faith. What I have provided in the preceding pages are ways that teachers who root their pedagogy in good faith can, through small acts, contribute to this work of e-racing. While the interventions I have suggested are provisional, it is my hope that colleagues can, in their context, improvise ways to continue this work. In the seeds of teaching in each of our classrooms we create new possibilities, not only for today's learners but also for future generations of the faith.

# Called Out My Name, or Had I Known You Were Somebody . . .

## THE PAIN OF FENDING OFF STEREOTYPES

### Nancy Lynne Westfield

*What are the experiences of racism and sexism in the theological classroom that are debilitating, paralyzing, and death dealing to Black women faculty, and why are they so? What if racism and sexism are disrupters of pedagogy in a Black woman's classroom? What is the cost of this disruption to her personally, spiritually, and professionally?*

## INTRODUCTION

Teaching is about stepping into, creating, and influencing multiple worlds. By virtue of racist privilege, when white teachers teach they are creating and influencing worlds where they are in command and control. The authority of their knowledge and capability is routinely accepted by students who enroll in their classes. In comparison, the worlds Black teachers attempt to teach into existence are compromised, controlled, and eclipsed by white students' power and reality. Teaching by Black professors is often contorted into reinforcing the construction of whiteness rather than the intent of rethinking, or healing, the construction of whiteness.[1]

My concern rests with the struggle of Black women professors who have chosen to teach in colleges, seminaries, and graduate schools. For us, too much of our teaching work involves fending off the racist stereotypes foisted upon us by white students (and students of color covetous of whiteness). The multiple worlds that Black women professors attempt to construct are often at odds with or must resist white domination and the hegemonic reality. White students bring their racist intentions, their racist naiveté, as well as their limited experiences and stereotyped understandings of Black women when they enter the classroom of Black women. The truncated imagination of white students, unwilling or unable to challenge and critique the stereotypes of Black women, becomes animated and energized as they enter our classrooms expecting Black female teachers to be contemporary versions of Mammies, Jezebels, Sapphires, or Superwomen. White students approach Black women teachers, signaling with their demanding and condescending attitudes, disrespectful behavior, and sullen words that the Black woman teacher is expected to be as their stifled experience has scripted, that is, to conform to caricatures as depicted by their unexamined racist thoughts. Black, Hispanic, and Asian students, complicit victims of the hegemonic reality, often follow suit with their self-indulgent behavior toward Black women faculty.

## FOCI OF THIS CHAPTER

In this chapter, I will focus on issues of African American women, knowing that African American men must contend with similar, if not the same, trouble. I am concerned with these questions for this essay: What are the experiences of racism and sexism in the theological classroom that are debilitating, paralyzing, and death dealing to Black women faculty and why are they so? What robs us of our passion to teach? What atrophies the maturation necessary for becoming master teachers? Why are there days when I feel as if I need combat pay just to show up on campus? What does it mean to heal from the wounds inflicted upon her by the academy, in general, and by students, specifically? What if racism and sexism are disrupters of pedagogy in a Black woman's classroom? What is the cost of this disruption to her? In this essay, I will recount two incidents that I believe point to the subtle and the blatant oppressive attitudes and behaviors that are commonplace for African American women professors to negotiate and endure. The first incident involved students of many races, and the second incident involved an African American woman student. I will give analysis for each incident, separately, then, because I believe that domination and oppression in the form of racism and sexism is at the heart of each incident, I conclude the essay with a pedagogical reflection for the survival of Black women professors. As I begin, I need to comment on my writing style. I am aware as I write I shift, without warning, between the first-person singular and the third-person plural. I am also aware that I mix analytic-prose with poetic-narrative. I, on occasion, also lapse into venting. I understand that for some readers this style of writing is confusing—disconcerting. I write in this unorthodox fashion (or perhaps womanist style) as a way to signal that I am deeply cognizant of the "insider" view I bring to my scholarship on Black women as a Black woman—"I" am writing about "Us." I also do it as a way to symbolize that my deeply personal voice and my scholarly voice are very closely aligned—maybe inseparable. I hope that my prose, analytical and poetic, will be described by all as an experience of vulnerability, which has moved them to rethink old thoughts and risk new actions.

*Called Out My Name (First Scenario)*

While it is, indeed, many years since desegregation and school integration, for the overwhelming majority of my students, I am, if not the first and only, then one of the few African American women teachers in their lives. More distressing, I dare say, is that I am one of the first and only Black women with authority and power over them in their lives. My students may have had African American women as maids or housekeepers, seen us in the marketplace or on TV. There has been, no doubt, the occasional friend of a friend who was a Black woman, but suffice it to say, the majority of these relationships have not been with a Black woman in authority and certainly not a Black woman with authority over them. My students signal their unfamiliarity, even discomfort, with this newness through behaviors that could easily be identified and dismissed as social faux pas. However, I find their behavior to be insidiously racist and sexist.

Without fail, every semester, beginning in the fall of 1999 and true to date, I am mistakenly called by the name of one of the other Black professors on faculty (there are five Black professors—three male and two female). On four separate occasions, by four different students, I was called by the name of my Black, male colleague. Sometimes I corrected the student, and sometimes I did not. Sometimes the student realized the error, most times not. No student has ever mistakenly called me by the name of a white professor—male or female. I have never been mistakenly called by the name of the dean or the president. A few semesters ago a student handed in an essay. While writing the student's grade in my grade book I noticed that on the title page of the essay the name of my Black, female colleague appeared rather than my name. I circled her name and wrote "Whose course are you taking?" Another semester, while co-teaching with a Black, male colleague, a student insisted on merging my name with my colleague's name—creating a kind of hybrid name. She created one name to simultaneously identify the two of us. This annoying behavior continued until my colleague firmly suggested the student stop. The student responded to his chastising request by saying she was just joking.

## Reflections on Scenario One

My hunch is that this pattern of student behavior is not social faux pas or lighthearted joking. Mistakenly calling me by the name of one of my Black colleagues points to the racialized perspectives and stereotypical categories that many students bring to the classroom concerning my race and thus my identity and authority. I am labeled, like my other Black colleagues, as "one of the Black professors." The students, in this name exchange for Black faculty, are signaling that we, as Black faculty, are somehow an amalgam or aggregate of Blackness—a wad of Blackness, interchangeable with one another, none distinct from the other, all about the same.

By categorizing us as "Black faculty," students exercise their privilege, their power over us. Using their power they are able to demand, control, and challenge us who are marginalized, thus enabling students to behave as if the Black faculty were in their employ, their workers, as if we are members of their personal staff. The pejorative label connotes the student's attempt to use the established and entrenched societal strata of prejudice and oppression to relegate those with the label of "Black" as inferior and powerless. Those lumped under the heading of "Black" then are understood to lack authority, possess an inferior status, are considered lacking by the academic community—in their own classroom. Regardless of credentials, employment status, tenure, scholarly prowess, or intellectual achievement, students, Black and white, signal that when the teacher is Black, they, the students, are in charge in the classroom because the faculty person's status would make the possibility of their authority implausible, even impossible.

The name changing and labeling that is foisted upon Black professors is a reminder to the students (of any race) that the racist strata of the larger society are to be adhered to, rather than challenged, in the microcosm of higher education. Their name changing, name creating, misnaming, and labeling are efforts to maintain the status quo that silences, degrades, and marginalizes Black, women faculty. Ideally, it is hoped that classrooms become places where power and authority are earned by intellectual achievement. The name changing indicates that Black women are at the margins in society and at the margins in their own classrooms.

If in labeling me a Black woman somehow meant I was able, wise, and powerful, this naming or labeling would be to my advantage. But alas, no. My hunch is that this categorization carries with it most of the historical baggage, assumptions, stereotypes, and distortions given to the category known as "Black women." This labeling is detrimental, as it is quite clear that in this racist, sexist, classist, exploitative, imperialistic society the label of Black woman relegates me to being inferior and mindless. The problem is not that I am called out of my name—that is the least of my worries. The problem is that once I am labeled "Black woman" and the meaning of "Black woman" rests upon the historic, negative stereotypes, students expect me to fulfill the roles of these stereotypes. Students, using their truncated racist imaginations, demand that I mammy them. Students expect that I will be the great mother-nurturer able to suckle away all their hurt and discomfort. From the students' vantage point, they are needy and I am obligated, duty-bound, compelled to fulfill their needs. Students come with the expectation of being mothered and are angered when they do not receive constant nurture and constant care. Students are surprised, even dismayed, when I set high scholastic expectations and requirements.

The national, racial, and historical hallucinations of Jezebel, Mammy, and Sapphire are embedded and deeply rooted perceptions of Black women that are in the conscience of the United States since slavery, and that are actively in the conscience of the students who enter my classroom. The responses to Black women professors are connected to the historic way Black bodies have been gazed upon, read, and used. If I am viewed by students as "Black woman professor," then these portrayals are their reference points. Students cannot help being confused when, instead of being met in the classroom by Miss Kizzy or Aunt Jemima or a prostitute, they are instead met by a scholar/pastor who wants to teach them the theory, tenets, and practices of religious education.

Stereotypes of Black women relegate us to a body with no mind whatsoever. The expectation of students provides for only two roles for Black women professors—either we are working bodies as domestics and mothers or we are hypersexual bodies. In either case, we are mindless beings valued only for the labor our bodies provide. As professors we are in larger contexts that suggest that professors and professing is a job of the mind. I can only imagine that encountering a Black woman professor is a major contradiction of terms and norms, so much so that it creates for students a kind of cognitive dissonance. For students (of any race) encountering a mindless being in a job that requires a mind, and then realizing that this mindless being has authority over, ability to grade, and the expectation to influence, is, at best, confusing, and for some, disturbing. Before enrolling in my course, the notion of a Black, woman scholar for most students was an oxymoron. Heretofore, a Black woman with a mind and with sanctioned authority was inconceivable and unimaginable. As students grasp for clues to interpret and bring meaning to this newly encountered reality, they default to what they know; they default to the stereotypes of Black women and inflict upon me behaviors that attempt to maintain and sustain their previous reality. These hallucinations[2] are particularly useful to white students as they are then able to remain in their narrow, racist comfort zones, able to maintain the stereotypes without critique. The hallucinations become a repository of what they cannot or will not accept about Black women—we are beings with minds, bodies, and souls; we are, as they are, human. The students signal their unwillingness to consider new relational metaphors for living beyond domination and oppression. The hallucinations are proof that white America, even in the early twenty-first century, can live apart from people of color so that the occasional encounters of Black women in classroom settings are still novel, still unusual, still not part of their normality. White students have few metaphorical categories for conceiving of and traversing a non-white world. Reality for them must maintain whiteness as the supreme norm.

## Had I Known You Were Somebody . . . (Second Scenario)

Approximately six years ago, in a spring semester, I taught a course on urban ministry. Twenty-seven students enrolled in the course—twenty-six were African American and one was Latino. Over the weeks, the students grew to be a cohesive group. The students were deeply engaged in new learning and insights—with the exception of one African American woman student, about forty years old, whom I will call Pat.

Much to my frustration and worry, Pat performed all the "bad student" behaviors: She was late for class, absent from class, distracted and uninterested in the conversation during class, participated in class conversation without having read course materials, turned in assignments late or not at all. Regardless of my efforts to reach out to Pat, her performance in my urban ministry course was less than mediocre.

The following fall semester, I sat in my office and Pat came in, greeted me with a smile and a warm hello and, without invitation, sat down in the chair across from my desk. Pat made small talk about the summer's activities and I sat in silence, still not sure what was going on or why she was now speaking with me. Pat took note of a book on my shelf—*African-Americans and the Bible*, edited by Vincent Wimbush (2000). Her expression grew animated. With excitement, she said that she had learned that summer that I had a chapter in the book. Cautiously, I nodded my head yes. Continuing in her conversation, she said to me, in a warm, affirming, even complimentary tone, I quote, "Had I known you were somebody, I would have done better in your class."

*Reflection on My Encounter with Pat: Black Female Patriarchy*

Now, six years later, I am still haunted by Pat's statement— "Had I known you were somebody, I would have done better in your class." Though this example is startling, I do not believe it to be an exaggeration of the severity of the problem between Black women. I think Pat articulated what many, many Black women think about one another—particularly about those of us who teach in the male-dominated world of theological education, ministry, and church. My encounter with Pat, I would argue, is symbolic of that which is killing Black women and paralyzing the Black community, that is, Black female patriarchy.

I have yet more questions: What does it mean when a Black woman student rejects the teachings of another Black woman because the professor is a Black woman or, more to the point, not a man? If Black women elect only to learn from men, choose only to take note of the leadership and the thinking of men, choose only to legitimate the work or words of men, what hope is there for our Black children, male or female? What does it mean when a Black woman student refuses to fully engage in a course that a Black woman professor is teaching under the proviso that the Black woman could never be "some Body" from whom learning ought to occur?

In this part of my reflection I will lean heavily upon the work of Alton Pollard III, especially in making use of his unpublished essay "A Woman's Work, A Man's World: Critiquing and

Challenging Patriarchy in the Black Family." I am arguing that the problematic of this case is, at the core, patriarchy, but much worse than patriarchy. I believe that what is at work in this scenario, to the detriment of teacher and student, is what Pollard calls Black female patriarchy. To understand Black female patriarchy, we must first understand patriarchy. All of us know what patriarchy is, so I will define it as briefly as possible.

Pollard, quoting Candace Jenkins, defines patriarchy as "the rule of the father, including the rule of older men over younger men and of fathers over daughters, as well as husbands over wives."[3] James Brown, late musical virtuoso, captured patriarchy when he sang the song, "It's a Man's Man's Man's World," which included lyrics such as:

> This is a man's, a man's, a man's world
> But it wouldn't be nothing, nothing without a woman or a girl.

My hunch is that the violence of patriarchy and misogyny is only exceeded by the devastation of internalized patriarchy by African American women. For me, this is the crux of this scenario, internalized patriarchy, or, as Pollard calls it, Black female patriarchy, at work in the relationship between Pat and me. Pollard defines his coined term as, "Black patriarchal male role idealized. Female patriarchs are not uncommon. Often occurs, but not always, in the absence of a male patriarchal figure; Hidden in plain sight, among the most ardent defenders of strict gender roles and expectations."[4]

Black female patriarchy is what happens as African American women take ownership of male domination, and participate actively in maintaining and supporting the power and privilege of men to rule over, exploit, and debase women. In trying to illumine the distortion of Black female patriarchy, I have tinkered with Alice Walker's definition of *womanist*[5] to further describe a Black female patriarch:

A woman who hates herself and other women, sexually and/or non-sexually; Has no appreciation and no preference for women's culture, women's emotional flexibility (believes there is no value in tears, believes that the counterbalance to laughter is fighting and warfare), sees women's strength as a threat to men and male power; Committed zealously to the exclusive survival of men and all that is male even if it means the denigration and debasement or annihilation of women and children.

Patriarchy is at its quintessential utmost when Black women use their power, influence, energy, and love to teach other Black women and Black children to be subservient to men, to favor male domination, to submit without question to male authority, abuse, and exploitation. As champions and victims of Black female patriarchy, Black women (we!) will fight other Black women, regardless of the physical presence or absence of men, to sustain the stronghold of abusive maleness with reckless disregard for herself, her own well-being, the well-being of her Black sisters, or the well-being of the entire community. In other words, Black female patriarchy, so complicit and compromising of the Black communal spirit, is the complete participation in the downfall of the Black woman and the Black community.

Having defined and described the terms necessary to frame and interrogate my argument, let's return to Pat, who, had she known I was somebody, would have done better in my class.

What terrifies me most about this statement by Pat is her inference that her learning was predicated on my body parts. It is fascinating to me that she did not say "had you been someOne," or "had you been someThing." She said "someBody."

I want to quickly raise three dimensions for the issue of body. First, I suspect that had my body been the body of power, authority, position; that is to say, had my body been male, then I would have been, for Pat, someBody. Without a male body I was no-Body. What I heard her say was that she would have chosen to participate more in the course had I had a penis. Pat made it clear that the absence of a penis was an obstacle to her being able to see me as an authority figure; I was, after all, not a man.

Second, an equal challenge to her misogyny was the fact that I am a woman. My colleague Arthur Pressley reminded me that fear is a major component of domination and internalized oppression. In this case of Black female patriarchy, Pat was threatened by me because my embodiment in the classroom is as a woman—a powerful woman. The presence of my female body only served to threaten and intimidate Pat—to make her fearful. I did not have a penis, and maybe worse still, I do have breasts—I do present to the world and my students a distinctively female body. I am five foot eleven, called "high yellow," at the time I was thirty-eight years old (younger than Pat), and I possessed a round, voluptuous, large body—to be more specific, I wear a "double D." I spend time and resources grooming and adorning my body, bringing attention to my body. I do not try to sexualize my appearance in the classroom. I am keenly aware that my appearance is part of my classroom and I dress with teaching in mind. When I enter a classroom, however, I do not leave my "double Ds" outside. When I enter a classroom, I enter as a powerful, commanding presence as teacher/scholar/minister.

I heard Pat say, in her backhanded compliment, that she could learn from me only if I *were* a man *or* only if I were *not* a woman. Regrettably, this means that Pat will *never* learn from me. Pat will never participate with me in the teaching/learning enterprise because I will never be a man, and more to the point, I will always be a woman.

And third, Pat indicated that if (maybe since) I was sanctioned by a man, then I might be able to be recognized. When she discovered I was associated with a man, in this case Vincent Wimbush, in her mind I was legitimated, made real, made authentic. Spending a semester in my classroom did not give Pat the kind of information she needed to validate my authority or authenticity as a teacher/scholar. Carol Duncan, scholar and friend, noted in a recent conversation that the words that I wrote and published in a scholarly text, a body of work edited by a Black man, took primacy over the words that emanated from my living, breathing Black, female, double-D body. I only came into existence through the words that were put on the printed page. Dr. Duncan said that had there been no text edited by a man, I would have had no body. My embodiment and selfhood as "text" was more present to Pat than her embodied encounter of me as teacher/scholar. The irony is, of course, that she, like me, inhabits the negated and dismissed body of an African American woman.

# THE PERIL OF A RELATIONAL PEDAGOGY

Colleagues have told me that it is my womanist pedagogy that invites these kinds of encounters. Womanist pedagogy espouses, at its core, the fostering of an incarnational milieu as the teaching/learning environ. It is a relational pedagogy. Womanist pedagogy teaches toward human-ness, that is, word becoming flesh.[6] The learning environment, the responsibility of teacher and student to tend and nurture, honors and respects the entire context of the person—mind, body, and spirit. As a relational enterprise, the teacher (albeit with experience, expertise, and authority) and learner (with experience and power) are co-learners struggling to hear and understand each other and the subject at hand for the healing, redemption, and liberation of all. The teacher and learner are challenged to foster an atmosphere of nondefensiveness so that barriers of power that reinforce oppression might be destroyed or reconceived. There is a climate of expectation that fosters the will to know and the will to become in both teacher and learner. Teaching is not politically neutral—it is, as bell hooks has said, a practice of freedom. Teaching and learning are politically charged as the awareness and responsibility of power dynamics are part of analysis and creativity. Foundational for good teaching practices is the facilitation of critical conversations that include connections between the personal narrative and larger societal issues.

As a womanist pedagogue I am disturbed by the issues in these scenarios because I believe, at their core, they are encounters of "dis-carnation," flesh becomes words; flesh objectified and wounded. Students come as experts of a pedagogy of domination—experiences where flesh is objectified and commodified, and minoritizing of the stranger is the norm. Flesh as words, the reading of my body for the maintaining of dominance, my body as pedagogy for the unrelenting construction of whiteness and privilege, the inscribing of their truth upon my bones is painful and potentially not only debilitating, but in direct contradiction to my espoused pedagogical values and constructs. What happens when a relational pedagogy is too wounding to practice? A classroom fraught with the dehumanization of racism and sexism is a battlefield or a graveyard or both. Black women teachers are shattered and broken due to the constant challenge of authority and the forced identity that is heaped upon us. Perhaps the use of a dominating pedagogy where students are silenced and merely recipients of information for memorization in politically neutral encounters would save much of this pain. What happens when sticking to one's values results in humiliation, harm, and trauma?

## CHALLENGING EARNED AUTHORITY— A PEDAGOGICAL ISSUE

The subtle and blatant behavior of students in both of these scenarios has to do with students challenging the authority of the professor. Students (of all races) too often challenge, not the content of my course, but my authority in the course. The unspoken questions in the room are: Who are *you* to tell *me* about this topic? or Who are *you* to give *me* a grade? The dynamics of the classroom is profoundly affected when the authority of the teacher is routinely challenged. These racist and sexist assumptions stifle the critical questions put forth by the syllabus. The privileged behaviors eclipse the creative questions that would potentially bubble up during class conversation. The attitude of oppression sours the climate of the course and hobbles my ability to teach.

The students' stereotyping me creates a reality in the classroom similar to the students viewing me through fun house mirrors. In seeing me as their indistinct version of "Black woman," they miss the real me, the genuine teacher, the truth-seeking scholar. When I am relegated to these stereotypes, I turn my body, my mind, and my spirit away from them in an effort to protect and defend myself and my craft. A relational pedagogy depends upon notions of authenticity and vulnerability from both teacher and learner. Vulnerability allows students to make connections between their own story and the subject at hand. Persons able to be authentic in the classroom push conversations to deeper levels of relevance, often giving way to better critical analysis and integration. Dialogue moves to deeper, more complex levels of understanding. Classrooms where authority is constantly challenged are places where the racist and misogynistic distortion prohibits the deep learning that vulnerability and authenticity would otherwise invite.

In the presumptive undermining of my authority the classroom becomes a place where true dialogue is eclipsed or perhaps impossible.

## FORCED IDENTITY—A PEDAGOGICAL ISSUE

Both of these incidents illumine the forced identity that Black women professors must resist, and to which many have succumbed. Black women are forced into the cookie-cutter personas of Mammy, Jezebel, Sapphire, or Superwoman, as if these one-dimensional characters could adequately capture the Black human drama; as if four garments created a wardrobe for every brown woman's body; as if four stars could capture the entire constellation of Black female-ness. Or we are forced to uphold female patriarchal notions that knot and contort or dismiss and disrespect our vocations and the best of our tradition. The identity of Black women, in general, and professors in particular, is complex and multifaceted. To make a template of her identity according to stereotypical possibilities is harmful and dehumanizing to her and sets her student up for an encounter of surprise and disappointment, even crisis. Black women who attempt to find ways of bringing their genuine selves into the classrooms, who decide that authenticity is critical for transformation of self and students, who attempt to resist the dehumanization of stereotypes and racism—these women are taking huge risks in their academic careers and daily lives. For the Black woman who decides not to satisfy the self-centered yearnings and voyeuristic curiosities of students, teaching becomes a death-dealing enterprise. It is death dealing because any efforts, reactions, or actions made to resist or refuse the neediness of students become part of the mythology of that faculty woman. Students, colleagues, and administrators use this information as a way of characterizing the female faculty person. The created narrative often reinforces the caricatured stereotypes. The narrative is often a way to characterize her as being hostile, mean, or simply unsupportive. (She is a bitch.) The cycle perpetuates itself when new students enter the school or when new colleagues join the faculty and the rumor mill is reactivated.

## THE SHATTERED TEACHER

Sustaining a womanist pedagogy has its price. Claiming and fighting for challenged authority and resisting forced identity takes an emotional, psychic, professional, and spiritual toll on Black women professors. The fighting takes huge amounts of energy. The cost of resisting these regular encounters is often a toll on her scholarship, on her family life, on her soul, body, and mind. Time that would be better spent on scholarship and matters other than survival is wasted. Battling about issues of authority and identity often renders Black women professors with a shattered and broken sense of self. It is no wonder that authenticity wanes or simply is not possible when the self is so wounded, damaged, and exhausted. In these situations, Black women must contend then with self-doubt and self-loathing. It is typical for victims of shame, humiliation, and violation to blame themselves for the attack or to take responsibility for care of the attacker. Routine attacks are often blamed on the victim, with some trying to convince her that had she done something differently this would not have happened to her. The violence that African American women endure in academic settings has misshapen our identities and goes unreported or underreported.

## NO PRESCRIPTION

My impulse is to conclude this article with the previous paragraph, but I believe that would feel irresponsible and unsatisfying to the reader. However, I do not want to fall into the trap of suggesting a prescription. A prescription, I think, would imply that the distortions and wounding nature of this reality are somehow not so complex or perhaps are even overstated. While I live in hope, I also know that institutionalized domination and oppression must not be trivialized or romanticized or ignored if Black women are to continue to survive in the larger society and the academy. I do not have a prescription for the dilemma I have just described and begun to analyze, but I am in conversation with women wiser than I about these ongoing and critical issues. I try to remember that I am not alone; pain will make you isolate yourself and feel sorry for yourself. I talk to Katie Cannon, Jackie Grant, and Delores Williams, depending upon them as the pioneering generation of womanist scholars, knowing they survived without a generation before them with which to consult. I talk regularly to colleagues in my generation, male and female, about the abuse and the wounds. And I try to support those women who are coming behind me into the academy and to talk to them about staying as healthy as possible and preserving their mental, spiritual, and bodily health. Above all else, I try to remember God and my own faith journey as I teach religion and assist pastors in learning for ministry. I believe what is most needed are multiple conversations on these issues. Multiple research projects concerning the impact and influence of race on religion and the theological classroom are needed.

# FIVE

# Reading the Signs

## THE BODY AS NON-WRITTEN TEXT

### Anthony B. Pinn

*What is the implicit and explicit significance of the body within the classroom? How might the presence of the physical body impact pedagogical considerations, particularly when the bodies are Black?*

Macalester College, during my years on its faculty, maintained an impressive diversity with respect to international students. Campus activities and conversations reflected this cultural difference and the "look" of the campus also made evident the representative presence of various segments of the globe—Asia, Africa, and so on. Less well represented, however, was the presence of students of African descent from the United States. And even the existing international diversity did little to mask Macalester's existence as an overwhelmingly white American institution. Classes, with few exceptions, reflected this reality, as it was highly unlikely that more than a few students of African descent populated any one room. This was the situation I faced in virtually all of my African American religions courses.

Even classes that were meant to revolve around lectures and discussion contained more than the information I provided behind the podium, or that was offered during dialogue. There was a larger and at times more imposing presence that also provided information—the bodies of those gathered. One experience in particular made the significance of the body within the educational process all too unavoidable.

I was a fairly new member of the faculty at Macalester College, but I had taught this course ("African American Religions") once before. And while things went well, in general terms, I wanted to alter class discussions and make them more engaging, more thought provoking. I wanted these discussions to raise hard and probing questions, to influence how my students thought about the course material. Students were involved in weekly discussion groups with the expectation that they would refine questions concerning course materials and explore answers within the context of conversation. This requirement was in addition to written work (e.g., reflection papers) submitted in a timely fashion.

## THE SCENARIO

Participation by students in class conversations tended to be somewhat bland. Limited personal commitment, limited ownership of ideas, and not enough attention paid to points of disagreement often marked the discussion hour.

I took into consideration that these were BA students taking an elective, with limited personal investment in formal religious life, and I recognized that they were of a generation with a different perception of religion's presence—in substantive or weighty ways—in the daily life of the United States. That is to say, they had a rather narrow definition of religion and its function. Nonetheless, the readings were provocative and I thought they, combined with lectures and students' questions, should spark more consistently engaged class discussions. The class size certainly wasn't a barrier in that the course consisted of roughly nineteen students. The racial makeup of the class was typical for Macalester—majority white American, many of those students having had limited contact with persons of African descent in and outside the classroom. The rest of the students in the class were of African descent—coming from various locations in the United States and the Caribbean. And I would venture to guess that for many of those students I was the first African American male teacher they had encountered during their life as students.

I decided to use the most heated segment of the lecture course—notions of religiously inspired social responsibility and critique as exemplified by Martin Luther King, Jr., and Malcolm X—to change the class discussion structure. I gave the students an extra assignment. I divided the students into two groups, one representing the thought of Martin Luther King, Jr., and the other representing that of Malcolm X. They were told to prepare a series of questions to ask the other figure and each group was to become familiar enough with the major components of their figure's thought to respond to such questions. Because of the racial makeup of the group, I gave little attention to how the students divided into groups.

On the day of the debate, the students sat in two groups across from each other, their body language relaxed. Things initially went well, and the first couple of rounds of questions got most of the students involved. But after the first fifteen to twenty minutes, things began to deteriorate as it became clear students were using this as an opportunity to "air dirty laundry," to attack other students using the King or Malcolm X persona as a mask. Body language showed tension. Those speaking began yelling, pointing—too many people trying to make a point at the same time. No one was really listening; they seemed too angry for that.

This dialogical devolution allowed for the worst aspects of "Minnesota nice" to manifest. From my perspective, "Minnesota nice" entails a mode of operation in Minnesota revolving around a pretense of cordiality that masks bigotry and so on—allowing disregard for others with a smile and without the looming threat of strong consequences. After all, the person who makes the prejudiced statement is "just kidding." Or, the person speaks so sweetly in front of the other that he or she is beguiled, only to later discover the "knife" in his or her back. "Minnesota nice" involves a preference for the avoidance of conflict *but* a tenacious attack once one's back is turned. It is a matter of seeking to do social harm incognito. The donning of the Malcolm X and Martin Luther King identities made such a situation more likely than I was willing to admit initially.

To use the assignment as an opportunity to feud over campus politics was not what I had in mind. The natural tendency to lament campus politics was intensified by the rather shadowy understanding of both King and Malcolm X for most of these students—both white and Black. They understood them, for the most part, through sound bites and warped depictions of King as the Christian leader whose dream was inspiring but rather non-threatening. The more challenging dimensions of King's political theology, particularly as represented in *Where Do We Go from Here?* were foreign. And Malcolm X was reduced to a single slogan—"By Any Means Necessary"—and a lopsided presentation of his social critique as "hate" speech. I asked them to dig deeper.

Things got heated and students were not certain how to respond. Those who were typically reluctant to speak closed down, and the more aggressive students became more animated.

Feeling a bit annoyed and confused by the developments, I stopped the exercise and explained what I saw as the strong points of the project—impressive preparation and involvement—and also highlighted what disappointed me: personal attacks and quick dismissals of different viewpoints. Many of the students didn't seem to "get" the point. They believed they had kept to the spirit of the exercise and assumed both Black and white students troubled by the exercise just did not want to deal with issues of race and racism. According to students holding this perspective, reluctance to deal with the "real" issue stemmed from Macalester's ethos as a "liberal" environment, overpopulated by well-meaning but do-nothing whites, and Blacks with limited race consciousness.

Students who were more typically quiet and reserved did not see themselves as reluctant to address issues of race and racism but believed the integrity of the process had been damaged and misused.

## BODIES: THE PROBLEM DEFINED

It took me some time to realize that the difficulty with this exercise was not limited to the intellectual issues at stake—the social theories and normative claims associated with each figure. There was also a more elemental, a more fundamental issue that was not expressed verbally. It was not simply their positions on King and Malcolm X but the force of their physical presence that mattered. The force of historical and cultural memory shaping and defining their physical bodies served to overwhelm their thoughts. The perspective and reaction of those in this classroom to the course material involved on some level the symbolic world of the body— the unspoken connotations of the "flesh." Although I did not initially recognize it, my pedagogy involved my conscious efforts to shape ideas through books, exercises, and so forth. But it also involved the unspoken significance of the bodies occupying the classroom space, and the bodies of those thinkers being explored, in conjunction with the bodies of my students. I would come to recognize that the pedagogical impact of physical and symbolic bodies on the learning experience is of as much importance as the course material.

While not always addressed in healthy ways, Black religious studies is familiar with the significance of the body within the context of religious doctrine, ritual, and activism. The manner in which the body houses and displays recognition of, wrestling with, and celebration of "ultimate concern" is the subject presented awkwardly in numerous academic texts, many of which have made their way into college, university, and seminary classrooms. However, in an odd twist, we seldom recognize the manner in which the body shapes the teaching of these dimensions of religious experience that depend on the presentation of the physical body. Although not articulated in sustained or creative ways, academic writing often acknowledges the embodied nature of our religious perceptions. Yet, in religious studies classrooms, the embodied nature of the learning process seldom shapes pedagogy in conscious ways.

While being mindful of the above, in this essay, I argue that the presence of the physical body in the classroom impacts pedagogy in that: (1) sociopolitical and cultural assumptions that influence the learning process are played out through the display of the teacher's body as well as those of the students, and in this way it is a non-written text that can trump written texts and organized exercises; and (2) the body, as a non-written text, can serve as an important resource in that it can be used as a way of introducing visual culture and the aesthetic dimensions of African American religion in ways that are not easily presented through the written text.

## HISTORY LESSONS: BARE BODIES

Students believe, in part based on what instructors with the help of admissions officers tell them, that the classroom is a "safe" space. To a limited degree this is true, in that students can expect to engage ideas, problematize them, or dismiss them, without the threat of *physical* violence. It is "safe" in that students can expect to enter and depart the classroom without being actively degraded, and so on. However, it is a space of duality—safe in some respects and threatening in others.

The exposure to ideas that decenter and challenge old assumptions and cultural preoccupations held dear poses an epistemological and, to some extent, an ontological threat or violence to self-perception, self-understanding, and a larger worldview. Nonetheless, we typically note the latter—this threat to or violence against self-perception and so on—as a positive dimension of the undergraduate and graduate educational process. It forges a space in which students are able to better explore, appreciate, and critique the social systems and larger world in which they live. We assume such a critical and engaged intellectual stance will yield practical fruit in that it will produce more reasonable and responsible world citizens. Yet, there is an underexplored and underappreciated dimension to this enterprise—a nonverbal dimension, a nontraditional text: the body. During this process of intellectual engagement, the body is usually a silent partner laid bare.

Some years ago Mary Douglas noted the manner in which the body is more than just a biochemical reality.[1] Certainly it is, but it is also a significant symbol of the social system in which it moves. The body signifies and also confirms the regulations and contours of the social system. Hortense Spillers gives this sensitivity to the body added texture by suggesting that a distinction must be made between the body and "flesh." It is the former, according to Spillers, that is the object of social attention—punishment and discipline as part of the inner workings of an unjust social system. The body in this sense is the "material" representation of the social system's inner workings, its logic played out in a visible form. The flesh, on the other hand, entails rebellion against the social system through the expression of cultural meanings that run contrary to the normative structures of the social system.[2]

As G. M. James Gonzalez notes when discussing Spillers's framework, the development of "property" in a broad sense involves the transformation of flesh into bodies.[3] That is to say, it involves the reification and objectification of what were culturally significant and "thick" entities. For our purposes here, the human becomes, through this devolution, a "substance" of limited value, limited visibility; or, in the words of W. E. B. DuBois, a "problem."[4]

It is an uncomfortable and unspoken recognition on the part of my students that resulted in the tension during that class exercise. As a matter of historical record they had some sense of how this tension of bodies played out during and before the civil rights movement. Martin Luther King and Malcolm X were powerful reminders of this. Although without the means to articulate it, the bodies of my students also knew this process—from differing vantage points, of course—and they responded. What they experienced on that day was a version of the psychological trauma described by Frantz Fanon on the day the white child noted his presence with a piercing remark: "Look, a Negro!"[5]

As the remark did for Fanon, the discussion in my classroom laid bare Black bodies, dissected them, and ripped them apart, exposing them, while reifying them—fixing them—within a certain existential, epistemological, and ontological space. This forced a reaction from both white and Black students, for differing reasons, of course, who considered themselves above the troubles that marked earlier ages—the pre-iPod and global cell phone ages.

It was difficult to be "politically correct" in the context of that classroom moment: Their bodies betrayed them, speaking a certain reality irrespective of the words issuing from their mouths. And my body only served to reinforce an uncomfortable reality: Differing values are assigned to bodies based on arbitrary factors. I had an intellectual sense that this transposition was a dimension, at least potentially, of the classroom experience, but I had not in this context given deep thought to how this was borne out on the practical level of my course, my lectures, my body. As a result, I was thrown, initially uncertain how to respond to having Black and white students learn through the presence of my body. Was this a "violation" similar to being profiled by law enforcement officers? Was this a natural component of the educational process, a dimension of what it means to take on the responsibility of teacher? The context of the classroom did not afford the time or space to ponder such questions. More recently I have begun to reflect on the manner in which bodies in general and Black bodies in particular are "worn" as masks that allow for sympathetic exchange but also that allow the wearer to hide, in that identity is concealed and information concerning that identity, that sense of self, is offered in a rather selective manner. There is little pedagogical value to this. However, "masking" can also involve an effort to learn the other. This is a more risk-filled endeavor in that it involves education through a deeper sensitivity to and understanding of how others view the world.

While beneficial, this process is far from problem free, as I came to recognize in my classroom.[6] The body speaks a world without uttering a single word. It is an intrusion promoting a rupture of social narratives, a visible sign and anti-sign of the colonization of knowledge. The result of this textual contestation is an epistemological dissonance.

These students, like most, had gathered much of their catalog of information concerning the world and its inhabitants from nonverbal markers and signs—the arrangement of bodies, normative aesthetics of particular bodies, and so on. Few of these epistemological elements of perception of self, others, and world were challenged in substantive ways prior to stepping on the campus. Mind you, I am not suggesting that my particular course was a life-altering experience as a unique part of the college curriculum. Rather, I am noting that the educational process at its best forces a confrontation with simple and complex structures of identity and identification in substantive ways.

Bodies were exposed, drawn out, laid bare; and students were confronted by the real-ness of those bodies and their experience of those bodies.

## THE BODY AS A NON-WRITTEN TEXT: A PEDAGOGICAL RESOURCE

The learning process should, drawing on the Spillers and Gonzalez formulation above, transform bodies back into flesh. That is to say, as a "religious" extension of their argument, the learning process should involve a thick recognition on the part of students and instructors of the details and inner workings of our world in ways that transform life. It should expose students and instructors to challenging questions and ideas that force a confrontation with the world—social systems, political and economic realities, cultural traditions, religious worldviews, and so on. And what better way to work toward this transformation than to highlight the reality upon which and through which these social and political arrangements, and so forth, are displayed and worked out—through the body as a non-written text?

It strikes me that the aim is to make visible the body as a pedagogical device and as a source of knowledge. Furthermore, such attention to the body in this capacity also highlights the general significance of "non-written" texts within the educational process. That is to say, assessment of information, the formation of "truths," is not simply the result of contact with written (second) texts, but also the body as first text.

In an epistemological twist, the body as source of information trumps secondary information as more readily acknowledged texts. Furthermore, the materiality of the body in various ways serves to bring into focus the unstated meaning of written texts.

While focusing on the learning experience within the context of Black religious studies, within the remaining pages of this essay I argue for three ways in which the body's significance for pedagogy might be highlighted: (1) attention to the placement of bodies in the classroom; (2) use of source materials that give priority to the way in which the body expresses religion and religious experience; and (3) assignments that require engagement with the "physical" dimensions of religiosity.

## PLACEMENT OF BODIES

Taking on the persona of Malcolm X or Martin Luther King, Jr., did not simply entail adopting ideas or accepting the legitimacy of abstract ideas. It also involved "possession" of new bodies—"bodies" socially, politically, and culturally marked in profound ways. I had given too little attention to the epistemological and ontological disruption this caused. I am not suggesting that such situations should be avoided. To the contrary, they can be instructive and useful pedagogical moves. However, this is the case when the connotations of this practice are recognized. Yet I had not given adequate attention to the dissonance created by the adopting of another's ideological consciousness within an already charged existential context.

White students were forced to "become" Black flesh, and in the process become—for many for the first time—aware of their whiteness, to own their whiteness and all it entails. And Black students were forced to add a layer of complexity to their Blackness, perhaps to think of what it means to be Black in new ways and in this way to feel the weight of their Blackness. Both potentially fruitful processes to be sure: An experience of a version of what DuBois recognized as "two warring ideals" in one body.[7]

I had the two groups sit across from each other. What this suggested for my students, I imagine, involved confrontation. Not the exchange of ideas but the proving of a point at all costs. I wanted the exercise to involve an exchange of viewpoints through a deep familiarity with the thought and ideological stance of each figure. Yet I failed to recognize how the placement of the bodies in the classroom fostered a more aggressive and less productive exchange than intended.

The assignment was useful, but it could have been more valuable if the placement of bodies had been consistent with the verbalized expectations. A circle, or perhaps a half-circle, would have been more conducive to the type of encounter I had hoped to orchestrate. That is to say, I set up the bodies in the classroom in a pattern of opposition: "you against me." And this arrangement of bodies served to jettison my verbal instructions in that the placement of bodies spoke louder than words.

SOURCE MATERIALS

Readings were helpful in that primary and secondary texts outlined and contextualized the course and provided basic information that would allow my students to understand and critique the courses' subject matter. Course discussions were useful at times. However, while these readings and discussions addressed certain abstract, de/bodied aspects of the subject, they did little to address the more ephemeral dimensions—the way in which the subject, the particular take on religion and religious experience, is shaped and defined through the way bodies occupy time and space—the placement, movement, and decoration of bodies.

Religion and religious experience are not simply thought. They are practiced, hence they involve an impingement on bodies—bodies in relationship to bodies and other visible and invisible substances. Such dimensions are not easily presented through the written word. For example, Ida B. Wells Barnett's descriptions of lynching are powerful, but they pale in comparison to the images of lynched bodies in the collection of photos titled *Without Sanctuary*.[8] Martin Luther King's sermonic pronouncements of the physical consequences of the struggle for freedom are, without a doubt, moving but not as moving as the images of young people battered by the content of fire hoses and bitten by police dogs. The brutal nature of these images that changed the collective mind of the United States during the civil rights movement also "spoke" in terms that supported Malcolm X's questioning of the dominant civil rights strategy. And the militant posture of Black Power advocates gave visual significance to the social theory and critique offered by Malcolm X in his various speeches.[9] Moreover, the energy and passion of spirit possession by the African god Shango or baptism within a Baptist church have been compellingly presented in numerous published articles and books. Yet the aesthetic quality of these events, the manner in which the body carries the weight of cosmic presence or spiritual transformation, is more graphically articulated through images captured on film, in photos, or through actual witness of religious ceremonies.[10]

Through attention to the body's role in religion and religious experience, both the thought and activity that mark these two are given more equal attention. Films, photos, Web-stream video, visits to religious communities, and so on all contribute to the creation of this pedagogical balance.

These non-written materials do not resolve ultimately the body dilemma; but I would not suggest such a resolution as the goal. The tension present in students' bearing the weight of their body within the classroom and beyond is instructive. This recognition of the body, however, is productive when students are given a way to address it, to learn from it. Words can only offer so much assistance with this goal and the rest must come through attention to the pedagogical implication of highlighting the body as a conduit for religious expression and as religious text.

## BODY-BASED ASSIGNMENTS

While in-class materials are important for recognizing the body's role in religion, the centrality of such materials may be noted through assignments that reinforce the merit of non-written texts as a part of the learning experience.

Of course, students can be required to view films, documentaries, and so forth, both in and outside the classroom. But highlighting the body's significance for the educational process by making such recognition a "gradable" dimension of the course can involve required field trips, for example, that combine observation, perhaps participation, and written reports. Demonstrations of religious activities, to the degree this can be done while respecting the traditions or movements highlighted by the course, also offer opportunities to highlight the body as religiously significant and as a viable text for the study of African American religion.

The challenge here is not so much the use of such assignments. Rather, the grading of these non-written text-based requirements poses a problem. How do instructors grade non-written text-based assignments when they have been trained to give priority to the written text? How does one assess the acquisition of knowledge in such cases? What does an "A" mean when the non-written text is highlighted? How is academic success measured in the classroom when "learning" the body, becoming sensitive to the role of the body in the fostering and living out of worldviews, is given a central place in the educational process?

On this issue I have more questions than answers. However, allow me to pose a possibility, one I hope to explore in my teaching.

Highlighting the non-written text allows, for example, ample opportunity for a multidisciplinary approach to the educational process played out perhaps through team teaching. For example, a course on African American religious experience might involve someone from a religious studies or history department who will highlight the more text-based dimensions of this subject while also highlighting non-written texts. And this person would be partnered with a scholar from the fine arts, for instance, who would highlight the manner in which the visual arts have been used to express religious sensibilities and practices. In terms of assignments, the more text-based scholar could take primary responsibility for written assignments (e.g., papers and exams) that involve attention to written sources of knowledge, and the scholar from the fine arts might take primary responsibility for grading assignments that are meant to have students recognize the religious housed within non-written materials. That is to say, assignments would allow students to explore through written papers and discussion the religious within written materials, and other assignments would allow students to wrestle with the religious in non-written materials.

The latter, it should be noted, does not require students to show proficiency as visual artists. Rather, in their written assignments, it pushes them to recognize the religious significance of the visual artist's work and to express this recognition in their written assignments and conversation. While this, I believe, is a useful practice, it does not resolve the primary importance given to the written text in that assignments continue to revolve around the production of written materials. Yet it does provide an important, albeit incomplete, push for pedagogical creativity.

Clearly, not all institutions of higher learning are set up for team teaching. However, where it is possible if not openly encouraged, the benefits are significant. Beyond providing a pragmatic solution to the dilemma of grading non-written assignments, this approach also highlights the importance of studying religion vis-à-vis multidisciplinary approaches. It allows for the development of synergies related to the study of African American religion by demonstrating the rather arbitrary and often politically contrived nature of departmental boundaries.

From this approach students gather an understanding of religion and religious experience as complex realities that require various theoretical and methodological tools.

When formal team teaching is not an option, this multidisciplinary perspective can also emerge out of conversation with scholars who are more familiar with analysis of non-written texts. Through conversation, perspective is gained with respect to how one might approach offering and evaluating assignments that highlight the nonverbal expression of religious sensibilities and practices. In this way the study of African American religion within the context of the classroom still benefits from the presence of an instructor sensitized to the significance of the body and other "nontraditional" texts.

Such synergy might inform not only the pedagogical dimension of the academic's life but also inform research. The latter might involve not only attention to the body for its religious significance but also the undertaking of more research drawing from the tools available in more than just one's own discipline. To some degree this is a common practice, at least implicitly so. However, there is a benefit to making it a more explicit and consciously undertaken practice. Questions, for example, related to theological anthropology and Christology, or church history, are given greater depth, and scholars have the potential of extending their audience to include scholars from areas of study that might not normally give consideration to African American religion because its study is typically too "theological" or too limited to flat historical description.

Finally, attention to the significance of the body for the study of African American religion—whether enacted through sensitivity to the placement of bodies, the presentation of bodies, or the development of assignments that center the body—adds thickness and "texture" to pedagogy. It allows instructors and students alike to feel the weight of the body and the manner in which this weight gives rise to creative approaches to ultimate orientation and ultimate concern. The centrality of non-written texts through attention to the body ties intellectual inquiry to all the senses. And what we come to realize is that "talking heads" do have bodies and these bodies, along with all the other bodies in the classroom, speak volumes.

# Emancipatory Historiography as Pedagogical Praxis

## THE BLESSING AND THE CURSE OF THEOLOGICAL EDUCATION FOR THE BLACK SELF AND SUBJECT

*Juan M. Floyd-Thomas and Stacey M. Floyd-Thomas*

*What does it mean for Black faculty persons to teach toward assisting Black students in overcoming the perceived conundrum described by Carter Woodson of the blessing and curse of Blackness? What might the development of an experimental model of pedagogical praxis that strives to engage, empower, and ultimately emancipate Black students look like, and what are the challenges and pitfalls of the model?*

More than seventy years ago, African American historian and educator Carter G. Woodson devoted serious time and attention to the importance of theological education within the African American community. Of particular concern for Woodson was the central relationship of African American education writ large and the Black church. Woodson leveled a scathing condemnation of the Black church for its anti-intellectualism, quiet complicity with social oppression, and faltering leadership, offering legitimate critiques that would hold equally true today. Yet, in spite of his condemnation of the Black church, he also praised the institution for its pivotal role within the larger Black community. Woodson stated that the Black church, as a whole, "has taken the lead in education in the schools of the race, it has supplied a forum for the thought of the 'highly educated' [African American], it has originated a large portion of the business controlled by [African Americans], and in many cases it has made it possible for [African American professionals] to exist."[1]

One might ask the following question about this obvious contradiction: "How can the Black church, with all its problems and flaws, also serve as the bedrock for education within the Black community?" In his classic work, *The Mis-Education of the Negro*, Woodson argues that

> in schools of theology [Blacks] are taught the interpretation of the Bible worked out by those who have justified segregation and winked at the economic debasement of [Black people] . . . to the point of starvation. Deriving their sense of right from this teaching, graduates of such schools can have no message to grip the people whom they have been ill trained to serve.[2]

This examination of Black theological education proves to be the most salient crystallization of Woodson's scholarly career and intellectual trajectory as an illustration of the ravages of Black miseducation. For Woodson, and countless other scholars since his time, it has been recognized that a vicious cycle is perpetuated for Black students in seminary and advanced theological education, wherein the pedagogical process is both a curse and a blessing. On the one hand, a theological education bereft of any substance and meaning for African American students is a curse because it will not only fail them as individuals but also compromises the churches, families, and communities that they will eventually serve. On the other hand, it is a blessing because a proper and meaningful theological education for African American students could render new visions of leadership and hope for the Black church as well as American Christianity writ large.

This chapter explores ways to overcome the perceived conundrum described by Woodson of the blessing and curse facing Black students and faculty within theological education. In taking on Woodson's challenge, we collaborated in an effort to develop a mode of pedagogical praxis that strives to be engaged, empowering, and ultimately emancipatory. Acknowledging this challenge, we accepted an invitation from a university other than our own to take part in an experimental four-day, thirty-five-contact-hour intensive course as part of a series entitled "God Talk with Black Thinkers." In that capacity, we taught an interdisciplinary course that we named "Contested Moments in the Black Experience: A Case Study Approach in Emancipatory Historiography." Twenty-three students were enrolled in the class, five of whom were from our home institution. Of the twenty-three students, there were nineteen Blacks, three Latina/os, and one Korean. When faced with what seemed like a once-in-a-lifetime opportunity, we believed from the outset, as many Black faculty often do, that if we could control the teaching-learning experience by creating a setting wherein all of our students were people of color and our course topics focused exclusively on the concerns and exigencies of people of color, then we would be able to ward off the difficulties concerning racism and other social ills that otherwise creep into our teaching experiences in predominately white settings. However, when given the chance to teach in such conditions, we soon found that nothing could be further from the truth.

We proposed the notion of emancipatory historiography as an interpretative framework for exploring Black racial-identity development in light of key controversial moments and events within U.S. history that have been generally ignored or rendered invisible within academic discourses such as the Thomas

Jefferson–Sally Hemings interracial affair, gay civil rights activist Bayard Rustin's role the 1963 March on Washington, the Anita Hill–Clarence Thomas sexual harassment controversy, and the recent case of the D.C. Beltway snipers as Black serial killers, among other issues. In an effort to deal with these issues, this course was designed to raise and fully discuss those questions of historic tensions and ethical crises that nonwhite people often wrestle with in silence and shame, especially topics such as the ones we mentioned that are so thickly interwoven with concerns about race, gender, sexuality, and power. From the very inception of this idea, we felt that whereas scholarly attention has been given to critical moments in the Black experience that have called witness to the social injustice that Black people have faced within mainstream American culture, little to nil of its analysis has entertained a Black-identified ethical perspective of the key turning points in Black historical and moral development. Thus, this course sought to move beyond the perception of Black racial identity as simply being, as Victor Anderson has so aptly named it, "the Blackness that whiteness created" and toward a worldview that is expressly defined by Black people with full consideration of their social, cultural, intellectual, and spiritual concerns.[3]

In this fashion, we wanted to offer a scholarly corrective to the normative gaze by looking at Blackness as an ongoing intracommunal project rather than an alternating politics of complaint and victimization. By emphasizing the coevolution of Black people's historical experience with their own moral development, we hoped to gain greater insights into an internally derived, representative impression of Black racial identity as the crossroads of private pain and collective reflections of morals and values that eventually provide the basis for indigenous communal expression.

In his acclaimed work, *The Souls of Black Folk*, W. E. B. DuBois asks a crucial question that specifically plagues African Americans but ultimately haunts all oppressed and marginalized people, namely, "How does it feel to be a problem?" For instance, one might ask what happens when the very thought of your existence as a person of color causes crisis and conflict within the broad sweep of the educational system in this country, regardless of whether you are student, faculty member, or administrator? Taking this issue further, DuBois offers a famous iteration of this concept wherein he asserts:

It is a peculiar sensation, this double-consciousness, this sense of always looking at one's self through the eyes of others, of measuring one's soul by the tape of a world that looks on in amused contempt and pity. One ever feels [a] twoness—an American, a Negro, two souls, two thoughts, two unreconciled strivings, two warring ideals in one dark body.

DuBois argues that the ultimate hope for resolving this tension is that it would someday be possible for every African American "to be both a Negro and an American."[4]

Within the experimental classroom dynamic that was already provided for us, the pedagogical strategies and concerns that we brought to the course were driven by a reciprocal notion of excitement shared by our students and us as teachers. Our excitement was fostered by the rare opportunity to test new ideas and principles in an academic context where all the members of the class were people of color. Conversely, the students' excitement—as best as we could discern—was largely fueled by the fact that they were in the presence of and being co-taught by a married couple of Black PhDs, a fact that cannot be overlooked. In addition, this scenario was further enhanced by a level of titillation based on the range of topics we planned to discuss during the course. Moreover, because this course was part of a unique curricular experiment, there was the shared freedom and excitement for both faculty and students alike in the realization that this teaching-learning experience existed beyond the pale of normal expectations and consequences that typically tends to bog down theological education. Nevertheless, no matter how and why this excitement was produced, the most pressing concern was what to do with it once we had acknowledged it as a factor in our teaching. As bell hooks discusses, the desire and willingness to set foot in a classroom with the intention to encourage excitement is an act of transgression. As hooks states,

> Not only did it require movement beyond accepted boundaries, but excitement could not be generated without a full recognition of the fact that there could never be an absolute set agenda governing teaching practices. Agendas had to be flexible, had to allow for spontaneous shifts in direction. Students had to be seen in their particularity as individuals . . . and interacted with according to their needs.[5]

By way of illustration, during the next to the last day of the intensive course, the sort of excitement that hooks speaks of, as well as the flexibility that it requires, provided us a fitting litmus test for putting such lofty principles into action. A student, we'll call her Jasmine, rushed back into the classroom after having been away for ten minutes in order to get a mid-morning snack so she could take her medication. Upon her return to the group, she began to recount a scenario that had just taken place in the nearby cafeteria wherein, after making what seemed like a benign request, she recounted how the male food service supervisor told her, "We don't serve you people!" As a Black woman, Jasmine instantly interpreted that statement as a racist verbal attack against her. She concluded her comments by saying, "After he said that, I knew I had to leave and share this with you all. I left immediately because what we're talking about in here is exactly what's happening out there." After the class took a second or two to recover from the shock of her statement, a Black male student, we'll call him Norman, responded, "I think we all should go with her and demand an apology." Noting the class's excitement and the event's relevance to that morning's class discussion on confronting racism through moral activism, we promptly gave the students a temporary break so that they could act according to their consciences. Without hesitation, the entire class left with Jasmine to confront both the offending worker and the head manager. The students demanded that the worker and his boss offer an apology to Jasmine and they refused to leave until she was satisfied by their sincerity. Once the two men came before the class and expressed how sorry they were for any maltreatment or misunderstanding, the students promptly returned to the classroom with a great sense of pride, vindication, and accomplishment.

Normally, such an "interruption" might be perceived as a chaotic outburst from a wild, unruly student. But it must be noted that, contrary to traditional views of the teaching-learning experience, the level of flexibility and adaptation in the face of such excitement should not be confused with a lack of preparation, foresight, or order on either the student's or the teacher's part. In fact, it is quite the opposite. Having a firm grasp of the content and concerns that would be broached during the class, there should be no fear that yielding to excitement is a corruption of the educational process when it is actually an enhancement of it, as hooks suggests. In order to embrace this generative sense of excitement and move beyond it, there is an intense realization within the classroom community that, according to hooks, "Our capacity to generate excitement is deeply affected by our interest in one another, in hearing one another's voices, in recognizing one another's presence."[6]

It would be foolhardy, however, to expect that every student in this group would share the same sense of excitement that was unleashed at that moment in equal or identical ways. As we witnessed the unfolding of a *sui generis* teaching moment, we understood that excitement, as with any outpouring of energy, can be either creative or destructive depending on the circumstances in which it is released into a finite space and time, such as what just occurred in the classroom. Such was the case with a student that we shall refer to as Eduardo who, although initially energized by the call to confront Jasmine's antagonist, soon retreated from his commitment upon discovering that the food service worker was a Latino like himself. Suddenly, his solidarity with this spontaneous quest for justice on behalf of Jasmine as a Black woman under racist attack was quickly held in contradistinction to his own feeling that a more natural ally was coming under siege by an uncontrollable surge of Black rage. To wit, even after the students sought no retaliation against the Latino food service worker, forgave him, and reconciled what they learned in class with their immediate experience, they were able to see this man—through Eduardo's intercession—as victim rather than oppressor. However, Eduardo was still reluctant to believe that the class could be trusted not to seek vengeance against this fellow. As a result, Eduardo's distrust led him to shut down and withdraw during the remaining day and a half of the course. This was evident in several ways: he no longer participated in class as freely as he did previously; he did not collaborate with his classmates on a required final group project; when his classmates tried to hold him accountable for not doing his fair share of the assignment, he questioned whether his fellow students' comments were retribution for the cafeteria incident a day earlier; and, most significantly, he directly questioned whether we, as the professors, could be trusted to discern the difference without allowing our race to cloud our judgment or harm his grade. In spite of our best efforts to hold him accountable yet also reassure him of our genuine concern for fairness, Eduardo was neither able nor willing to dismantle his internal scripts about who had power and how such power would be exercised. Thus, the blessing of excitement is often met with the curse of horizontal violence. The logic of horizontal violence among the oppressed and marginalized peoples within the classroom is, according to Paulo Freire, based on the reality that "the oppressed, instead of striving for liberation, tend themselves to become oppressors, or 'sub-oppressors.' The very structure of their thought has been conditioned by the contradictions of the concrete, existential situation by which they were shaped."[7]

This, in turn, was largely shaped by a fear of freedom set at the core of the psyche of oppressed peoples via an internalization of oppression as a normative societal script embedded within the educational enterprise at its myriad levels. "The oppressed, having internalized the image of the oppressor and adopted his guidelines, are fearful of freedom" because, in the words of Freire, they innately understand that "freedom would require them to eject this image and replace it with autonomy and responsibility."[8]

In light of Freire's freedom mandate and Woodson's identification of the Black theological educational context as a transformative space for both the self and the subject, we propose a fivefold pedagogical praxis of emancipatory historiography. The first central aspect of emancipatory historiography as pedagogical praxis is the validation of agency. Herein, we must be committed to the axiom that "no pedagogy which is truly liberating can remain distant from the oppressed by treating them as unfortunates and by presenting for their emulation models from among the oppressors. The oppressed must be their own example in the struggle for their redemption."[9]

For the true evolution as well as elevation of the subjugated and disenfranchised within our midst, they have to be able to see themselves as able to both pose and solve problems rather than to *be* problems. Following this example, in order for one to be an agent of change, one must become an agent of change.

The second aspect of emancipatory historiography as pedagogical praxis is that it is dependent upon creating a dialogical space that is free, fair, and fearless. "Founding itself upon love, humility, and faith, dialogue becomes a horizontal relationship of which mutual trust between the participants is the logical consequence. It would be a contradiction in terms if dialogue—loving, humble, and full of faith—did not produce a climate of mutual trust, which leads the people involved into ever closer partnership" in addressing the social ills that confront all people.[10]

In a dialogical space where love, humility, and faith are absent, the necessary prerequisites for a genuinely free, fair, and fearless teaching-learning experience are undeniably lacking.

The third aspect of emancipatory historiography as pedagogical praxis is the importance of reflexivity. In spite of our best intentions, many teachers seem to "forget that their fundamental objective is to fight alongside the people for the recovery of the people's stolen humanity, not to 'win the people over' to their side." To reiterate this key issue, ultimately it is the paramount goal of the emancipatory educator "to liberate, and be liberated" with the students—not to charm or entertain them.[11]

This dimension of our teaching approach operates very much in accordance with the traditional West African philosophical adage, "I am because we are." Taken further, the core belief in the reflexive nature of emancipatory historiography is the idea that the "learning process comes easiest to those of us who teach who also believe that there is an aspect of our vocation that is sacred; who believe that our work is not merely to share information but to share in the intellectual and spiritual growth of our students."[12]

The fourth aspect of emancipatory historiography as pedagogical praxis is the need of unity with as well as among the oppressed in creating a liberating teaching-learning experience. In the schema we propose, both the teacher and the learners must become aware that it is the intention of traditional modes of education to divide the disinherited as an undeniable ideology of oppression. Once again, Freire offers a vital insight when he states: "In contrast, achieving their unity requires a form of cultural action through which they come to know the *why* and *how* of their adhesion to reality—it requires de-ideologizing. Hence, the effort to unify the oppressed does not call for mere ideological 'sloganizing.'"[13]

A sense of connection for each person must be regarded as a deliberate call to remake the world into a place that is free, fair, and fearless and cannot simply be given insincere lip service.

The fifth and final aspect of emancipatory historiography as pedagogical praxis depends upon teachers and learners finding themselves situated within a mutual process of "bearing witness" as a means of critical engagement with the dominant society. Bearing witness, in this instance, takes on a deeper, more urgent dimension that entails the following: the consistency of words, thoughts, and actions; the audacity to risk everything in the quest for freedom, justice, and equality; the radicalization that occurs when the teacher and learners are able to speak truth to power; the courage to love one another into wholeness in spite of how and why we are broken; and the faith in the fact that, no matter what forces are arrayed against the weak and dispossessed of the world, truth fears no trial and eventually the truth liberates both speakers and listeners alike.

In closing, we know that this proposed schema is by no means a guaranteed cure-all for the wide range of issues and challenges that were reflected in either the theorized observations of Woodson, DuBois, hooks, and Freire or in our own anecdotal experiences in the classroom. Nevertheless, it is important to envision this notion of emancipatory historiography as a mode of pedagogical praxis that can potentially allow all participants in the teaching-learning experience to engage in the task outlined by Woodson all those years ago, namely, to transform ourselves as well as theological education into a relevant, life-affirming, and critically engaged social enterprise that seeks to offer all disinherited and marginalized peoples the ability to live our lives and tell our truths freely, fairly, and fearlessly.

# SEVEN

# Black Rhythms and Consciousness

## AUTHENTIC BEING AND PEDAGOGY

### Lincoln E. Galloway

*What is authentically Black? What does "being Black" mean for our existence as humans and our vocation as teachers? What kinds of pedagogies emerge when one is Black? What particular rhythms of consciousness give meaning to teaching and learning?*

## INTRODUCTION

This conversation revolves around the topic of being Black, teaching black in institutions of higher learning. To speak of being Black, teaching Black is to bring into sharp focus the realities of identity and practice that Black professors appropriate, cultivate, navigate, and negotiate across a spectrum of complex and dynamic realities that have implications for the teaching-learning event, the students, the curriculum, and the institution. These realities are conveyed through conversations, personal reflections, insights, and stories that reflect intimate and all-encompassing aspects of our very beings. In my view, to appreciate the Black professor's pedagogical practices (i.e., teaching Black) requires some awareness of the existential dimensions (i.e., being Black). One might say that such intimate engagement of a person's self-understanding goes to the very heart (and indeed, body—as other contributors will show) in ways that can be unsettling, affirming, death-inducing, or life-giving. Conversations about teaching Black are also conversations about being Black where the latter is best represented in terms of well-being, life, and death. In this chapter, I have chosen to spend some time with the construct "being Black" in order to show how pedagogy emerges from the core of the Black professor's being, and also to raise awareness of the dangers to the Black professor who attempts to separate pedagogy from the realities of being Black.

## BEING BLACK: IDENTITY, DIVERSITY, AND AUTHENTIC HUMANITY

When I began my reflections on being Black, teaching Black, I recognized, in the broadest sense, that it would require some understanding of my own being and also some engagement of those values or ideals that influence my pedagogical practices. As a Black professor with a Caribbean heritage, I had to reflect on my own roots, my worldview—in short, those elements that contributed to my own sense of identity. Indeed, my own self-understanding was shaped by a cultural landscape that was marked by the yearnings and struggles of Caribbean people around issues of identity and self-determination. Vera Bell captures this idea of consciousness and appreciation of one's own cultural heritage in her poem addressed to a forebear being sold as a slave at auction:

> Across the years your eyes seek mine
> Compelling me to look . . .[1]

Each passing decade of the post-slavery era has witnessed increasing and unrelenting waves of consciousness beating on the shores of the Caribbean countries and providing the impetus for the formation and transformation of a Caribbean identity. Each wave bore within it the forlorn echoes of indigenous peoples whose populations were decimated, whose cultures were erased, whose stories were replaced by those of European exploits acclaimed as discovery and enlightenment. Each wave engendered within Caribbean people an increased sensitivity and receptiveness to the distressed calls of a multitude of ancestors whose humanity was crushed and whose hopes and potentialities were extinguished. Each wave transported across the sands of time the memories of ancestors who shaped the islands with their presence, their stories, their spirit, and their impulses toward freedom and full humanity.[2] These waves of consciousness are constitutive of Caribbean identity, reflect its diversity, and call forth its full humanity.

It was, therefore, no surprise to me that my perspective on this topic of being Black, teaching Black would move in the direction of waves of consciousness, notions of identity in a context of diversity, and ideals of freedom and full humanity. Somewhat aligned to the last is the notion of authenticity: living out of one's authentic self and establishing authentic meaning and purpose in one's life. In my view, such a conversation has the potential to raise issues and questions, construct definitions and models, set forth new perspectives or directions—all of which go to the heart of one's being (and, indeed, body), as a Black professor. Increasing consciousness allows the Black professor to grow roots that lead toward meaning-making as one explores elements of Black culture in the broader global context.

## WAVES OF CONSCIOUSNESS: BEING BORN AGAIN

James Cone's story provides one perspective of a person whose journey toward consciousness was radical and life transforming. James Cone makes this case very strongly when he describes his own experience in coming to consciousness about his own Blackness.[3] This, for Cone, was when he was born again. Cone suggests that it was a great awakening that for him was more radical, more life transforming than anything else he had experienced in life. The Christian faith had been an enduring and constant part of his life. He had always accepted the God who loves, who is present in the person of Jesus, and who is able to make a way out of no way. This was his reality. It was all around him at home and in his church family. It remained with him through all of his theological studies. However, when he began more intentionally to engage Black culture, he describes himself as having been reborn—a born-again experience that was life transforming. Cone indicates that he had completed a doctoral degree in theology and still had not yet come to this awakening.

Cone's story is emblematic of the journey of many Black scholars whose theological education was not designed to reflect or engage their own cultural realities. Indeed, being born again into a consciousness of one's identity, and the rhythm of one's culture, does not always parallel or accompany one's journey through educational institutions. This reality is often very acute for Caribbean scholars who study outside of the Caribbean. Their education may have the effect of alienating them from their own people, the cultural rhythm of the land, and ultimately from themselves.[4] For me, being born again into consciousness of the rhythms of Black cultural life in the Caribbean was only one part of my reality. Living in the United States of America would require a constant struggle to determine how not to become alienated from the echoes of Caribbean life, alienated from my own cultural roots, my life's center, my identity, and my own humanity. However, it would also require consciousness of the rhythms of Black cultural life in North America. This constant experience of being born again into broader dimensions of consciousness has an impact on both my being and my pedagogy. The journey that informs my identity and challenges me toward greater authenticity as a

Black professor will inform the curricular offerings that I design for students.

A second area that is informed by growing waves of consciousness is the presence of diversity. The Caribbean reality is always that of encountering and reflecting diversity. The rhythm of the land of the earliest peoples, the Amerindians, was disrupted as a result of the overwhelming pillaging, plunder, and piracy that the European colonizers inflicted. Other discordant transitions included the introduction of the plantation system and the use of Africans as slaves. The landscape was scarred by this violent system and other foreign impositions of race, class, and caste distinctions. These impositions intensified with the later additions of Asians and East Indians to the cultural landscape of the Caribbean. Given this background, Wilfred Cartey points to the ways in which Caribbean poets and novelists trace the evolution of a social consciousness among Caribbean people and also the ways in which their writings reflect the rhythms of the crossing and intermingling of peoples of African, Asian, or East Indian descent that give rise to an amalgam of beliefs and practices.[5] The rhythm of the land that beats across the Caribbean cultural landscape reflects and promotes the rich vibrancy of diversity. Lucie Pradel reflects on the composite and diverse character of Caribbean cultures in terms of the interweaving of fabrics. Pradel traces the African influence in the pluralistic religious practices that support and preserve the memories of oral traditions through fundamental vectors of myths, rites, rhythms, stories, proverbs, songs, dances, and sculpture. However, she is aware of the multiplicity of contributions of each ethnic mosaic in the diversity of the larger and more panoramic "cultural *métissage.*"[6]

In the third instance, the waves of consciousness also give rise to impulses toward freedom and full humanity. Dwight Hopkins sets before us the ideal of having people be more conscious of the ideas' assumptions of self, culture, and race.[7] He points out that the vast majority of European American men rarely confess their racial identity in religious scholarship, whereas the naming is evident in the work of European American women, Blacks, Native Americans, Hispanics/Latinos(as), and Asian Americans. Hopkins suggests that among the latter groups the naming that is so evident is derived "from their celebration of racialized selves in order to embrace the beauty of the cultural particularities as contributions to a universal well-being."[8] In his view, we can move toward being human and support human flourishing as we become more aware of the ideas that have shaped our present context. Hopkins writes, "By making these realities and relationships more conscious, people can become more open about their ideals, about a good person, a worthwhile life, and human destiny."[9]

The Black scholar is claiming his or her identity and cultural roots but also helping others move toward a more complete humanity. From Hopkins's work it is clear that such pedagogical moves will require honest engagement of the self, of race, and culture. Cornel West also sets before us the ideal of our full humanity and destiny. West describes human connection as a constitutive element of prophetic thought. For him, there is a moral moment in always attempting to remain in contact with and never losing sight of the humanity of others. West highlights an essay by William James written in 1903 upon the occasion of the invasion, occupation, and annexation of the Philippines in which James raises the question of why it is that so many of his fellow citizens in the United States of America were unable to empathetically identify with Filipinos as human beings but rather cast them as stereotypical pictures and portraits.[10]

In this area, the pedagogy that emerges will be directed by the goal of helping others experience authentic humanity. This work toward recognizing the worth of all humanity coincides with the goals embraced by humanists in their quest to inculcate respect for nature, culture, and the arts, as well as "concern for humanity around the globe, demonstrated through efforts to ensure peace and health."[11]

The waves of consciousness shape our beings and we engage not only our own internal ideals but we also engage with institutions. Black scholars from the Caribbean, Africa, or other places within the African Diaspora teach and undertake scholarly pursuits in North America. We bring with us particular cultural rhythms that must engage the North American cultural landscape from the particularity of Blackness. As a Black scholar, I bring a Caribbean presence that goes to the core of my being. Wilfred Cartey speaks of presence as a cultural or spiritual term suggesting the person in his or her own spiritual interiority and selfhood bestowed by one's own people and embodying their values, mores, and worldview.[12] Caribbean presence brings the rhythm and vibrations of the Caribbean to intermingle with the melodic improvisations of Black life in North America. This is one dimension of being Black that is played out in academic life as well as the ecclesial and broader cultural landscape. In every context one has to negotiate and navigate through issues of identity, diversity, and humanity.

In my engagement with academia and my particular institution, I bring a Black presence that is shaped by my Caribbean identity, the reality of Caribbean diversity, and the quest for authentic humanity. For some of us, being Black, teaching Black is realized in the context of academic institutions that traditionally have been constituted by a predominantly (and sometimes exclusively) Caucasian presence in students, faculty, and administration.

In his work *Being Human*, Dwight Hopkins uses the fields of philosophy, anthropology, and missiology to demonstrate particular ideologies that create and sustain the very enduring systems of privilege and marginalization. The legacy of these theories and practices derived from these disciplines still lurks within our institutions and broader cultural life today with debilitating consequences. Philosophers such as the Englishman David Hume, writing around the middle of the eighteenth century, could declare "negroes and in general all other species of men . . . to be naturally inferior to the whites. There never was a civilized nation of any other complexion than white, nor even any individual eminent either in action or speculation. No ingenious manufactures amongst them, no arts, no sciences." Hume continues, "In Jamaica, indeed, they talk of one negroe [*sic*] as a man of parts and learning; but it is likely he is admired for slender accomplishments, like a parrot who speaks a few words plainly."[13]

The far-reaching consequences of this worldview from Europe to her colonized regions have had deleterious consequences for substantial numbers of peoples who do not claim European ancestry. The philosophical speculations of philosophers such as Hume and Kant were rarefied, reinforced, and reflected in the attitudes of those who shaped academic disciplines, as well as the political, economic, and cultural elements.[14] Others who held similar attitudes and worldviews felt it was their obligation to set out on Christian missionary endeavors to transport Christian values to places such as Africa and the Caribbean in order to share the civilizing effects of the Christian gospel. It was their belief that the Christian gospel could restrain from all that went with dark skins, dark hearts, and dark thoughts and deeds. Yet they remained certain that although the gospel had civilizing effects, it could not bring persons of darker hue along the spectrum of light to true humanity reserved only for whites. The vestiges of these ideological postures and the structures that have been built upon them are still with us today and need to be confronted in the institutions in which we work.

Many academic institutions of religion and theology now recognize diversity as critical to their identity, discourse, and practice. The rubric of diversity is only one discursive or practical avenue through which to approach the realities of being Black, teaching Black in non-Black contexts. In this conversation on being Black, teaching Black, personal and institutional realities are brought together in a particular configuration that may promote and enhance both personal and institutional health, effectiveness, purpose and relevance, and authenticity. Institutional commitment to diversity provides a doorway toward a new way of being, or of engaging, challenging, revising, and designing foundational experiences for more effective educational experiences in the twenty-first-century classroom.

# CONSCIOUSNESS-RAISING: FROM BEING BLACK TO TEACHING BLACK

Whatever their approaches may be, many academic institutions, such as theological schools or seminaries, recognize the merits and value of exhibiting themselves as communities that are open, inclusive, and diverse. The core commitment is generally to enable students to reach beyond their own cultural confines to develop a global sensibility that widens their horizons, and enables constructive engagement with people of all faiths and cultures. This commitment also requires pedagogical shifts that take seriously the plurality of cultures within the global village. In other words, among other things, pedagogy must contribute to the humanizing of our globe to bring dignity, shape values, and honor diverse identities in globally meaningful ways. Here, I share Dwight Hopkins's ultimate concern to see the dismantling of both the ideologies and the structures built on them that have allowed one group to control and dominate others.[15]

From my perspective, I ask the following questions: How can I facilitate increasing consciousness? How do I nurture and maintain an awareness of my own identity? How do I honor diversity? How do I embrace practices that call forth full and authentic humanity within me as well as others around me? The following pedagogical principles are proffered with these questions in mind.

I first observe that the work toward consciousness-raising is not always accomplished within accredited educational institutions. In some cases, educational institutions offer courses of study that lead scholars to experience estrangement from themselves and their cultural roots. This is the reality of many African American scholars studying in the United States, and that estrangement is further compounded for Black scholars whose cultural realities are shaped by other countries of origin such as those in Africa or the Caribbean. In such cases, the rhythms that beat to raise consciousness are experienced through deliberate or fortuitous encounters in conversations, extracurricular sources, and appropriate networking. Being Black, teaching Black requires this commitment from scholars to seek outside experiences within their cultural roots for their own health and that of the institutions they serve.

As a Caribbean person, I am aware of the struggles of Black Caribbean people to understand their African heritage and also to recognize the diversity of traditions that have contributed to a Caribbean culture. From this perspective, one can deduce that to honor the rhythms of life that reflect such diversity, the Black scholar must resist the inclination to abandon her or his own uniqueness by recognizing the alienating elements that coerce conformity, homogeneity, and sameness under some seductive metanarrative of oneness and unity. For the Black professor, the push toward sameness may emerge within Black communities that are not actively reflecting and engaging the heterogeneity that constitutes Black culture and experience across a broad spectrum. *The odd man out is always Judas.* However, this heterogenity is also likely to reflect the expectations of other ethnic groups that operate with stereotypical images of Black individuals, communities, or cultures.

## BLACK VESSEL AS REPOSITORY OF ALL THINGS BLACK

The Black professor will honor the rhythms of diversity by resisting sameness and pressing for diversity in the student body, the faculty composition, and the curricular offerings. Institutions are drawing attention to diversity as a selling point for their programs. Black professors are able to help their institutions achieve this goal as they respond to their own need for institutions to be more culturally diverse. However, this task requires vigilance and self-care since the goal of diversity should be an institutional commitment and not just the institution's goal by means of enthusiastic Black activists.

In reflecting on the issue of the expectations placed on Black faculty in predominantly non-Black institutions, one of the contributors to this volume remarked, "Why do I have to be the repository of all things Black?" In other words, institutions may be inclined to lean heavily on Black professors to respond to and provide insight into every situation that deals with Black people, their countries of origin, culture, and concerns. In such cases, the Black professor must guard against the danger of succumbing to institutional expectation to be the expert vessel of all things Black.

## STUDENTS WHO HAVE NOT BEEN BORN AGAIN CANNOT LABEL OR NAME

Black professors may find themselves in contexts that seem to conspire to wage an assault on the mind, the body, and the very being of the professor. In these contexts, professors have to be particularly aware of the responses that will render their pedagogy ineffective and have debilitating effects on their being. One such context is encountering students who (to echo Cone's testimony) have not been "born again"; in other words, students who have not had to examine the ideological underpinnings of the world that they inhabit and the assumptions that currently shape their academic disciplines, preferences, and intellectual lives. In some cases, these are European American students who may have understood themselves as the ones who name or label reality. The Black professor whose pedagogy may seek to raise consciousness of alternate perspectives may find that students are suspicious of any method, design, approach, or model that has not emerged within the mainstream of the discipline.

Undoubtedly, the Black professor must be constantly aware of the contexts that students might receive with suspicion or distrust. The lack of trust of one's pedagogy or lack of respect for a person's work has the potential to create negative energy in the classroom. In the case study, the professor's passion, preparation, and pedagogy are treated with disdain and with a dismissive demeanor. In such cases, a teacher may have to be prepared to develop strategies in the classroom that will lay the foundation or anticipate responses that are inappropriate. Since there are students who understand themselves as the ones who label, define, name, or determine what is significant, these students will also assume that there are no consequences for their own responses if they dismiss, disengage, or disrespect the work of the Black professor.

## STUDENTS ON INTELLECTUAL SAFARI MUST DISEMBARK

The Black professor who invests intellectual capital, time, and effort in designing lectures, modules, or entire courses cannot afford to have his or her work treated with disdain or disrespect. The professor may sense a greater need to establish classrooms as laboratories where ideas, assumptions, questions, or assertions are taken seriously and students are held responsible for their thinking. Such experiences may be difficult for students who resist lectures, modules, or courses that engage (or honor) the work of persons who have traditionally been marginalized. Courses that invite students to see the world from a different perspective, or in which the students find that their experiences are not normative, or in which the status quo is challenged may be uncomfortable, for some students are unwilling to face the issues that are raised. However, students do not have the luxury of becoming spectators or treating the course material as one does a video or souvenir of some exotic destination. In our conversations, one of the contributors to this volume described this luxury as "voyeuristic spectatorship" and noted that students should not be allowed to go on an "intellectual safari." From the occasional lecture or course to the entire design of the curriculum, students are not being well served if they can conveniently avoid material that is designed by professors who are being Black and teaching Black.

## TOXICITY AND THE TENETS OF TEACHABLE MOMENTS

In spite of a teacher's best efforts, there will be teaching moments that are disturbing, peculiar, and sometimes so negative that they may be toxic. These occasions can no longer be viewed as teaching moments. The teacher recognizes that in spite of one's own training and expertise, one's familiarity with the material, one's preparation, one's passion, some students have crossed the line. The student makes a derogatory remark about Black people, Black women's bodies, Black religious life, Black intellectuals, or the like. The student may choose to invade a Black professor's personal space, or act in ways that are demeaning, hostile, or condescending. Nothing about this interaction can be defined as a teachable moment when one has been violated. Responses by students that diminish who we are serve to negate the potential of teachable moments. Some of these occasions may arise simply because students are faced with disturbing pedagogy. One hopes, in such moments, the professor may be able to recognize clearly (even if one is unable to articulate): "You have violated me, my life, and being, and this is no longer a teachable moment." The professor must pay attention to her or his being if pedagogy is going to be effective. In short, an event cannot be a teaching moment when it diminishes who we are as Black people (academics or professionals) and as human beings.

AUTHENTICITY VERSUS IMPOTENCE

The teacher does have the option of allowing the classroom experience to degenerate into an endless cycling and perpetuation of destructive energy. The teacher participates in this syndrome when she or he internalizes the negative energy of students and determines that her or his work is not important. This rejection goes to the very heart (and body) of what it means to be a Black professor. The issue of Black bodies (especially women's) is dealt with elsewhere in this volume. However, Black bodies can also reflect the stress and pain of teaching in an environment that is too toxic. (In one of our conversations while working toward this volume, one participant opined that an unusually high number of Blacks in academia have suffered serious medical conditions that may be caused by the stress of "teaching while Black" in particular educational institutions.)

Black professors must focus on being Black since it is the basis for teaching Black. It is also at the root of institutional life, classroom interactions, engagement, or conflict. By this I mean that cultivating one's own identity and authentic humanity is at the heart of well-being and productivity. How does/can your teaching style handle those moments when your very person or being is under attack? The danger here is that the Black professor may not have adequate tools to deal with rage—internalized rage—that renders one impotent. One must be careful not to accept the state of affairs or participate in one's own oppression or demise. For true humanity to flourish in others, the Black professor must continue to cultivate it by cherishing the rhythms of consciousness that call forth work that is vital, critical, and indispensable.

For me, Being Black, Teaching Black is about developing strategies for moving toward more authentic humanity. Pedagogy with a commitment to move toward authentic humanity takes seriously the stories of many and diverse peoples who have been marginalized, colonized, or dehumanized by powerful others. Such pedagogy will address and take seriously such global concerns as the exploitation of human resources, global violence, and conflict, and allow persons critical space for engagement and creative theological construction. In other words, an awareness of oppression and dehumanization will evoke particular rhythms of consciousness and commitments to pedagogy that provides for naming, challenging, and struggling with the identifiable dimensions of oppression in our world, our texts, our institutions, and our practices.

# THE ABSENCE OF LUMINESCENCE

Assuming that the Black professor conceives of theological education as a transformative enterprise, the professor will approach the task with clear goals. The narratives, conceptual frameworks, and practices in the classroom will indicate a commitment to justice, and be predicated on the goal of transforming values, knowledge, and practices. However, even the best pedagogical practices designed intentionally to challenge students to engage the textual materials with intellectual rigor in an environment of openness and respectfulness may be met with resistance.

Pedagogical practices may require recognition on the part of the professor that certain classroom dynamics may generate instability, disruption, and resistance as students confront themselves, the teacher, and the material in the context of the classroom. This is necessarily so since to question and be questioned in one's foundational worldview is always unsettling and threatening. Teaching Black will require pedagogical practices that deal with students who have been socialized to understand themselves as those who name and label reality. Such pedagogical practices may have to confront the power that lurks or tries to conceal itself under the larger narrative of diversity.

Elsewhere, I described the loss of Black faculty and the courses they teach as the absence of luminescence within the institutional life that results in a black hole.[16] However, the term can become a metaphor for the personal and professional life of the Black professor whose being comes under assault and for whom authentic humanity is no longer a goal. The alternative is internalized rage, impotence, a sense of despair and meaninglessness, a loss of dignity and respect, and, ultimately, a loss of self and being (Black).

## CONCLUSION

The Black professor moves toward authentic humanity by paying close attention to the waves of consciousness, the shaping of her or his identity, and the connections and responses to the cultural rhythms. Paying close attention to one's being will translate into pedagogical practices that will contribute to human flourishing and well-being. This may mean that pedagogical practices may have to be designed in ways that do not permit or reward distrust, dishonor, or disrespect of the professor's labors, scholarship, and competence. These pedagogical methods cannot contribute to, support, or encourage "intellectual safaris" or "voyeuristic spectatorship."

The presence of cultural diversity and even a school's public comments in support of this diversity do not erase or conceal the systems of dominance with which some students identify and may even seek to exploit. Black professors must be mindful of the struggle with and for power that may detract from the underlying goals of confronting the demons of dehumanization, as well as the commitment to bring about change consistent with human dignity and wholeness within a diverse global village.

In being Black, teaching Black, there will always be a need for Black professors who, both in the classroom and in the larger institution, are exercising proper self-care, allowing themselves to be born again with increasing commitments to human diversity and authentic humanity. The alternative in the form of internalized rage and impotence takes away one's humanity and threatens one's well-being and life. It is an alternative that for the Black professor may result in, dare I say, "Lights Out!"

# From Embodied Theodicy to Embodied Theos

## Stacey M. Floyd-Thomas

*What does it mean for Black women professors to claim authority and respectability in the classroom while refusing to be seen as a mammy or a menace? What happens when, even before she utters her first word in a classroom, her Black female body is the most contested and embattled aspect of the teaching-learning experience? To what extent are Black women's bodies the proverbial battlefields for the so-called "culture wars" in this society, and how can a cease-fire be declared?*

I could list several scenarios and scores of real-life case studies torn from the text of my own teaching experiences that speak to the perils and dangers of teaching while being Black and female. I could recount several scenarios about students who could see me only as sister, girlfriend, mama, daughter, lover, Aunt Jemima, Oprah Winfrey, or the Black friend they never had. Or I could expound on the stereotypical stories about students who saw me as their own personal *bête noire*—because for them I was "too Black," "too mean," "too intimidating," "unnurturing," or "emasculating"; in other words, they saw me as the *big Black "bitch" that they love to hate.* But regardless of such a litany of offenses and near misses, as well as the messiness of deciding which ones to choose to list here and those I'd leave out, I see them all converging toward the same moral crisis of my embodied theodicy as a Black woman professor in an increasingly white and male academy. For many of my students, and even some of my colleagues, I am always something other than Dr. Stacey Floyd-Thomas, a seminary professor, for as Patricia Williams states of her own embodied presence in elite, white, male spaces: "no matter what degree of professional I am, people would greet and dismiss my black femaleness as unreliable, untrust-worthy, hostile, angry, powerless, irrational, and probably destitute."[1] Consequently, I am never allowed to fully or freely be myself because of the sheer weight of other people's stereotypes, illusions, fantasies, and self-deceptions.

## CONTESTABLE ETHICAL ISSUES

What are the peculiar experiences of embodiment for Black women? How can Black women claim authority and respectability in the classroom without being seen as comforter or combatant? What do you do when your pedagogical delivery, course subject, or theoretical orientation is appropriated or used by students as a vehicle for self-disclosure or an impetus for sexual discovery? What defenses or offenses must Black women use in order to ward off illusions of intimacy? What happens when, even before you utter your first word in a classroom, your physical body is the most contested and embattled aspect of the teaching-learning experience? To what extent are our bodies the proverbial battlefields for the so-called "culture wars" in this society and, if so, how can we declare a cease-fire?

## EMBODIED THEODICY

Also described as the insufferable quest to exert one's inherent aptitude and goodness in spite of society's stereotypical claims that a Black woman represents the incarnation and existence of evil and inferiority, embodied theodicy is rooted in an existential crisis for Black women in the academy. As a contemporary update of

W. E. B. DuBois' trenchant vision of the Black experience, I am asserting that we as Black women in the academy face an inner turmoil that amounts to nothing less than an embodied theodicy that results in a divided consciousness. In this regard, the Black woman is a sort of scorned stepchild, born with a veil . . . in this American white and male academy—a world that yields her no true self-consciousness and no body-right, but only lets her see herself through the revelation and desire of another world. It is a death-dealing sensation, this divided-consciousness, this sense of always looking at one's self through the eyes of others, of feeling a stranger's eyes become words become flesh that slaps or molests you at whim, of measuring one's success by the tape of a world that looks on in repulsion and lust—a Black woman's body; a white-trained mind; two souls, two thoughts, two irreconcilable strivings; two warring ideals that are torn asunder morning by morning and day by day.[2]

All of this taking place amid an ongoing struggle to simply pursue her call and vocation to the utmost of her ability relatively free of harassment, antipathy, and abuse in implicit or explicit form. Very often, the ramifications of this divided consciousness manifest themselves in devastating ways: the nagging fear that, even though you are good enough to excel at the task, you might be unable to prevail against the odds; the loss of (or the desperate search for) any meaningful human relationships; unresolved resentments about the proverbial Faustian exchange you felt forced to make between your high-priced education and your peace of mind; interminable health care scares and crises that wreck our bodies when we cannot resolve the crises plaguing our minds.

## THE SUPERWOMAN-VILLAIN DICHOTOMY

Caught within what womanist ethicist Katie Cannon has called a "superwoman-villain dichotomy," Black women professors are forced into ill-fitted and ill-named boxes that serve as either a means to professional suicide or real-life coffins.[3] When a Black woman professor insists on being taken seriously as doctor, professor, scholar, and colleague, and thus refuses to assume stereotypical roles, focusing explosively on the formal tasks of her job, remaining rigid in her avoidance of personal involvement, isolating herself and making herself unavailable for informal contacts, she's deemed and labeled as a "villain," carrying the image of a cold, inflexible authority and "Bad Earth Mother." Hers is the lot that must deal repeatedly with the dependency of students' fear and rage that is covertly and overtly expressed while she becomes deluged with the petty requests for the unceasingly needed clarification of students who find her simple tasks too difficult to understand and her teaching style too cold to warm up to, so that when she's not besieged with hostile challenges in and out of the classroom from the students, she spends the remainder of her time defending her authority, autonomy, and academic freedom in the dean's or president's office.

Or, as Cannon tells us, we can go the other route and become superwomen—veritable Oprah Winfrey carbon copies who are subjected to our students turning our classes into talk shows and forcing us to become the surrogate for their every need, comforting the weary and oppressed, interceding on behalf of those who feel abused, championing the cause for every student at her own expense, compensating for the deficits of our other colleagues who are unable or unwilling to teach, speaking up for those who are unwilling or unable to speak for themselves, making demands on their behalf; doing more than our share of work to make up for students and colleagues who refuse to complete their assigned task or teach any lesson; becoming the Mother Confessor to all—expected to counsel and advise students on matters unrelated to the tasks at hand and always willing to use our bodies and lives to protect the seemingly innocent and dampen the aggression of others.

# THE COMMODIFICATION OF OTHERNESS

To fully appreciate the brunt of embodied theodicy as divided consciousness for Black women professionals in a postmodern era, the role of the Black woman academic is the prime location that both publicly declares and perpetuates the idea that there is pleasure to be found in the acknowledgment and enjoyment of Black women's bodies, regardless of their intellect, status, or authority. As bell hooks warns us in *Black Looks*, this "commodification of Otherness has been so successful because it is offered as a new delight [in the academy], more intense, more satisfying than normal ways of doing and feeling"—teaching and learning.[4] Within the conspicuous consumption and commodity culture of the ivory tower, Black women professors become spice and flavor, much like a metaphysical Mrs. Dash, if you will, seasoning that can liven up the dull dish of the mainstream white curriculum or larger Eurocentric heteropatriarchal learning machine. When a Black female professor such as myself enters the classroom, a reality inversion occurs: For the students, the outcome and objective of the course is their desire, her body becomes the text from which they fulfill their objectives, and her evaluation as a teacher becomes based upon her ability to fulfill their fantasies and not her ability to convey information or teach them to learn. Whereas all professors contend with the consumer mentality prevalent in current pedagogical encounters and experiences, it is, however, the Black woman professor who contends with the fact that it is her very physical presence that is consumed, with the expectation that it should taste spicy and flavorful, but not be intelligent, informed, or knowledgeable. Thus, regardless of her intention, regardless of her villain or superwoman role, she's not her own but forever commodified as a spectacle to be seen, felt, and touched and as an incidental "other" or condiment on her students' palettes. They know whether we are present, but they never allow us to be fully potent or poignant.

The crisis in constructing, or in this case reconstructing, identities emanates from the nagging questions of "Who am I within this process?" and "What is happening to the me I know myself to be?" Unfortunately, the learning machine process of getting into graduate school, getting a job, getting tenure, and getting promoted oftentimes results in the foreclosure of a Black woman's identity when she didn't even realize that she had taken out a mortgage on her soul. More than that, this perennial paper chase overrides conscious efforts as well as the necessary time toward reflection and self-examination for Black women professors. Indeed, the more Black women aspire to become credentialed in institutions of higher learning and acquire the requisite cultural capital, the more external judgment becomes integrated into her fundamental self-identification. DuBois would most likely look upon this situation and state that true self-consciousness would rarely be attainable for the Black woman scholar. Indeed, when we suffer through the systemic abuses and internalized symptoms of this embodied theodicy, it can often lead us to cry silent tears in a lonely room while asking God the simplest, most human question: "Why must I suffer like this?"

The eyes of this white and male-dominated teaching-learning realm become the normative gaze that penetrates every facet of our lives—physically, psychically, and spiritually. One of the most fundamental purposes of the normative gaze is the constant assault on Black women's dignity. Subjected to the tyranny of a white heteropatriarchal norm, Black women as professors might be likened to a battered woman caught within the panoptical gaze and omnipresent purview of her violent lover. Even when she is safely removed from her batterer, she is obsessed by the controlling gaze of her abuser. She rises early to see how she's going to dress for him. She speaks little of her discomfort. She cuts off healthy interaction with anyone besides her batterer, claiming that they wouldn't understand what it means to be her. She blames herself for any mishap she encounters.

# EMBODIED THEOS

At the heart of womanist pedagogy exists the only possible remedy to embodied theodicy, that is, embodied theos. According to Cannon, the basic motif of embodied theos is the use of writings of Black women as testaments and road maps for how to endure, survive, and overcome the projections of racist misogyny. These road maps are often found in the work of Black women novelists such as Toni Morrison, Alice Walker, or Zora Neale Hurston— works of art that explore Black women's bodies as social texts. According to Cannon, the normative project of Eurocentric patriarchy and the death-dealing toll of enlightment and theology have been built upon, drilled into, and buttressed against the foundation of Black women's flesh. If we want to dismantle the master's house that has stood for centuries on the backs of Black women, we must read the text that has been written by Black women's bodies. In her publication entitled "The Womanist Theology Primer—Remembering What We Never Knew: The Epistemology of Womanist Theology," Cannon uses Morrison's book *Beloved* as an example. At the heart of *Beloved*, Cannon says, is the mind of the slave,

> the mind that carries the memories of the body, the memories of . . . women and men "moved around like checkers." During chattel slavery children were . . . sold . . . at such a young age that the mother had not formed memories of them. . . . Morrison says that the way in which we remember is by taking a slice of history and undeliberately trying not to remember. Remembering is no less than . . . the experiences of our bygone days re-embodying themselves in our . . . flesh. The theme of embodiment as re-memory

and re-memory as reincarnation is the basic motif in embodied theos, a major concept in womanist pedagogy.[5]

Embodied theos entails rendering personal experience in the lives of individuals and groups in specific times and places in ways that are essential to justice-making transformation. Such renditions have to be both *discrete*, in terms of their particularity, and *concrete*, in terms of their palpability. By so doing, each of us unmasks the veracity of our circumstances by means of recognizable modes of identification. It is important to indicate how, with embodied theos, seminar discussions can be configured so that critical dialogue regarding the "personal as political" is constantly reasserted and reinstated.[6]

By way of example, in the womanist classroom, reciprocity is a central pedagogical element; every member of the class must participate. In any learning environment that is bound to have wide differences of opinion and sharp contrasts in social realities, all students must mutually engage the course of study and their classmates so that they can cultivate their own ethical voices and begin to develop methods and frameworks of moral reasoning that will prepare them to face any situation. The irreducible character of the common language we develop in the confines of the womanist classroom as well as the dynamic forces that affect our conflicting realities, intra- and interpersonally, is what makes personal accountability so pivotal to the formal/formative concept of an embodied theos.[7]

At the heart of embodied theos for Black women professors is to read our own bodies and the terrain upon which we walk within the academy and the classroom—a foreign terrain when realizing that our students go through cognitive dissonance when we walk into the classroom and our body goes through an untold series of shocks when we enter contexts we cannot transform to our own living conditions. If in this educational endeavor and career trajectory we seek not to abort the gifts we have been blessed with and trained to carry, we must be straightforward, up-front, and bold-faced with the discombobulation that our students experi-ence when we walk into the classroom. We cannot numb up or dumb down in order to become neck-up thinkers, barefoot enter-tainers, nor remain as strangers in a strange land. We must not use our bodies but rather our embodied theos as the backdrop for our teaching-learning experience—allowing the contextual nature of learning to facilitate a process that will allow others to cross boundaries with care.

A means of resolving bridging the gap between embodied theodicy and embodied theos is possible. Public intellectual and social critic, Michael Eric Dyson has offered an intriguing matrix for understanding representations of identity development for Black people in contemporary society that I would like to appro-priate for the work of moving Black women from an embodied theodicy to an embodied theos. Within Dyson's discussion of racial politics and identity formation, he asserts that we must be cognizant of the stages, styles, status, and strategies of Blackness. These stages of Black identity development, according to Dyson, "refer to how Blacks dynamically negotiate offensive, misleading or troubling information about Black life."[8] For the purposes of a womanist standpoint these stages are:

*Stereotype:* White prejudiced and misogynist beliefs and bigoted intuitions are dressed as objective observation and common sense.

*Archetype:* The projection by Black women of what we believe to be the defining characteristics of our identity as a marker for self-determination of self-definition.

*Antitypes:* The expression by Black women of the irreverent meanings of Black female intellectual identity that transgress against accepted norms or beliefs.

The styles have to do with seeing Black culture and identity in either complex, dynamic terms or simple, absolute ones. The sta-tus of Blackness is done in the hopes of wrestling with the thorny concerns of Black authenticity ("keeping it real" in hip-hop jar-gon) within Black culture steeped in a strictly positive versus negative dialectic. Finally, this leads to strategies of Blackness that determine how Black folk manage their identities ontologically. In other words, strategies concern how we as Black people offer the world a picture of our Blackness. The strategies are as follows:

*Accidental Blackness:* We are human beings who, by accident of birth, happen to be Black and female.

*Incidental Blackness:* We are proud to be Black women intellectuals but we are so much more.

*Intentional Blackness:* We are human beings who are proud of our integrated selves as womanist pedagogues who see our Blackness as a critical yet integrated element of our identity/consciousness.

In sum, the strategies of moving from embodied theodicy to embodied theos are seen as a means to permit Black women to negotiate the white or male world while remaining sane, balanced, and maybe even at peace in this cruel, callous, and cold world (or at least classroom).

## CONCLUSION: SO WHAT?

To be Black and female is not to be subjected to a divided consciousness but to be knowledgeable of two worlds—to know what one is doing and the reasons one is doing it. Yet being Black and female creates conflict. But only conflict creates awareness. Awareness brings about change. Change may actually induce social justice in and through itself. Being a Black female scholar and teaching in the white male academy can be an act of becoming an agent of social justice. This act insists that one must take charge of one's life by embracing conflict in order to break with past habits of corruptive notions of civility, casualties of honesty, illusory intimacy, and virtual realities.

To be an agent of social justice is to answer the ethical questions of who we are and who we ought to be by appreciating the role our personal identity has within reality. I teach my students that only what we do reflects who we are, and who we are shapes not only the world in which we live but also our personal life chances. Therefore, our quest to be safe, free, and rid of anxiety, and to experience conflict resolved is directly linked to our own reflexive behavior as we seek to become moral agents of social justice. This clarion call of conscience at such a critical and uncertain time as this, I tell my students and I reassure myself, is the ultimate urgency that causes us to immerse ourselves into what life has to offer before our time runs out and our life chances end.

# Teaching Black

## GOD-TALK WITH BLACK THINKERS

### Arthur L. Pressley and Nancy Lynne Westfield

*What does it mean for a Black student to learn about issues of faith, theology, and leadership in a white institution? What type of curriculum prepares Black seminarians to be effective and competent in the local church?*

Thurgood Marshall and the NAACP, in an effort to challenge the Jim Crow laws, targeted the U.S. school system and the notion of separate but equal. Arguing before the Supreme Court, Marshall, using the work of noted social psychologist Kenneth Clark, suggested that the U.S. educational system was based upon a color caste system that caused irreparable harm to Black people. Known as *Brown v. Board of Education*, this landmark 1954 decision has brought increasing numbers of Black students into predominately white schools. Since that decision, there has been significant legal and political discussion about strategies for achieving racial equality, while there has been proportionately less attention paid to the curricular needs of African American students in predominately white schools. With this inattention to curricular needs, African American students attending predominantly white schools have felt that they were either invisible to white teachers, had to become white themselves in order to graduate, were unfairly targeted by white teachers as inferior students, or were attacked for attempting to express who they were as people of color. African American students in predominantly white schools also struggle in conflictual relationships with African American faculty persons. These relationships often are filled with clashes as neither Black faculty nor Black student knows what to expect of each other in a predominantly white context. Black students express frustration that faculty hold them to a higher standard and Black faculty feel disappointed when Black students come to class unprepared and insist that class time be spent reflecting upon issues of struggle, oppression, and personal harm.

Any attention paid to issues of Black students in predominantly white schools has been subsumed in the conversation of multicultural education that has burgeoned in the last twenty to thirty years. The movement toward multicultural education has sought to make schools more welcoming to students regardless of their ethnicity. This movement's goals have been the ending of racial discrimination while teaching people to be more racially sensitive. The movement has sought to make school more welcoming to students in general or to give white students a more "diverse" experience in preparation for the changing workforce. Not only is there an assumption that all students learn the same, one assumes that the outcome of learning is the same for all students and should be the same for all students. Despite these noteworthy goals, the aims of multicultural education have failed to speak to the particular challenges of African American students. While multicultural education is a trend with significant impact upon the educational system, it has failed to take seriously the relationship of curriculum and racial identity and thus the impact upon African American students. Multicultural education does not attend to the needs of racial identity and the unique historical backgrounds of African American students.

# ASSUMPTIONS AND PRESUPPOSITIONS

This chapter assumes that African American students in general, and African American theological students in particular, have unique pedagogical needs that must be addressed when they are attending predominately white institutions. A presupposition of this article is that a fundamental need of all students is to have their racial, gender, and social identities affirmed. The affirmation of social identity must occur before true learning takes place. In the past, issues of identity formation were the implicit agenda of programs like African American studies, or women's or Asian studies. These programs served to create space for discussion where students could wrestle with their social identity under specific intellectual rubrics. Another example of aspects of campus life that supported social identity is Black fraternities and sororities in white schools. In white schools, Black Greek organizations provided much-needed venues for racial, emotional, psychological, and social identity in the confines of a fraternal community.

The focus of this chapter is on theological education. The problem of identity is more acute when it comes to theological education. The curriculum of theological education requires the engagement of a number of questions that go beyond other kinds of education. Such questions include, What does it mean for a Black student to learn about issues of faith, theology, and leadership in a white institution? What type of curriculum prepares Black seminarians to be effective and competent in the local church? These questions must be grappled with in any context, but especially in predominantly white seminaries where there exist implied benefits that are derived from sitting next to white students. Questions about the racial and professional identity of the pastor and congregation must be addressed in the curriculum of white seminaries, while the issues concerning the education of Black students in predominantly white schools have had little research.

This chapter is a description and analysis of The God Talk Project, which was developed at Drew Theological Seminary in 2002. This project began with the concern of two Black professors discussing the need for Black students to be more aware of their intellectual and cultural history. The colleagues believed that clergy must see their intellectual tradition in correlation with the social and political needs of their community. The model, called God-Talk with Black Thinkers, informed by womanist thought, engaged pedagogy, liberation theology, and psychological theory, and began as a series of intensive courses that experimented with issues of introducing Black students to the wealth of African American scholarship. The project then moved toward having the students use Black intellectual scholarship to think critically about the needs of the African American communities. Part 1 of this chapter recounts the story of the project's genesis. Part 2 describes some of the component parts and how the project functions at Drew. And Part 3 provides psychological and pedagogical analysis and reflection upon the learning theory of the model.

## PART 1: THE GENESIS AND ARTICULATION OF THE PROBLEM

*James Who? A Lack of Knowledge*

The "God-Talk with Black Thinkers" project had its beginning one afternoon in the seminary coffeehouse. While talking with an African American student, Professor Arthur Pressley suggested that *Black Theology and Black Power*, by James Cone, would be essential to the essay the Black student was writing on liberation theologies. The response of the student was to ask, "James who?" This moment began a conversation between Lynne Westfield and Pressley about the current state and needs of African American theological students at Drew University. It was clear that Black students not only had no idea about James Cone, but that they had little critical knowledge of liberation theology or black theology. As we reflected on their discourse in class, and their sermons and papers, especially as these related to the African American community, we became acutely aware of a number of deficits. Namely, that they possessed limited understanding of the wider field of theology and other related disciplines, particularly as these disciplines assisted them in thinking about the lives of Black folks, and the experience of the Black church. Black students were unable to bring to bear the richness of Black intellectuals and theological reflection on the needs of African Americans to address structural problems of domestic violence, racism, poverty, HIV/AIDS, substance abuse, and the long list of other social, political, and spiritual concerns. Students who are unaware of the major thinkers in their community are not able to think critically about the lives of African Americans. Critical analysis requires that students have multiple perspectives to investigate a problem, and yet that these perspectives share some common goals and cultural assumptions. Students learn multiple perspectives from being aware of what others have said about the problem they are investigating. More important, our students, symbolized by the question of "James who?" did not know how to think critically about the ontological reality of Blackness in a scholarly, critical way. Without this ability, they are unable to design and implement ministries that will bring about healing and growth in Black communities. For the most part, the students were rather parochial in their approach to problems, typically offering solutions that have already been tried and that had failed to bring needed change. Such students are unable to develop ministries in their churches and communities that facilitate spiritual and emotional growth. Most students enter seminary with unhealed personal wounds from social and childhood traumas. Until they have encountered a healing community in the process of their education, it is impossible for them to imagine how to provide this for others.

*James Who? An Antiquated System*

The problem of "James who?" is a problem that exists not only at Drew but throughout much of theological education. The fundamental question confronting theological education is about training students to use traditional and contemporary intellectual thought in organizing for change and to move communities into new paradigms. In order for students to use theological and philosophical thought to facilitate change in communities, they needed to have experienced change themselves. The problem for most theological schools has been that most students graduate thinking much like they did when they started seminary. Students graduate without a clear understanding of pastoral ministry. They have not spent significant time developing their approach to social policy or developing insights into the nature of the good community. The curriculum, for the most part, does not provide opportunity or time to foster ideas about creating healthy families, healthy relationships, or healthy congregations. It is not that traditional courses in church history, the Bible, church administration, and pastoral care are not taught—on the contrary, they are taught in precisely the same manner that they were taught decades ago. Theological education remains unchanged for the past six or seven decades while the church and the world has drastically changed. In short, the current approach of theological education courses fails to grapple with the lived reality where the students will practice ministry.

*James Who? An Issue of Liberation*

To state that students are unchanged by theological education is to argue that they are unredeemed by the process. The problem of unredeemed students, "James who?" students, is more than a problem of course content or the failure to use intellectual traditions to think critically about social issues. The problem of unredeemed students is, at its core, an issue of liberation. Students need the experience of liberation if they are to be a liberating presence in their communities. The current approach values the re-creation and perpetuation of systems of oppression that further harm members of their congregation and community.

# PART 2: THE MODEL

## Administrative Support

Pressley and Westfield proposed to the dean of the Theological School a model that would be a series of intensive courses. The courses were designed to put Drew seminarians and graduate students in dialogue with some of the best African American minds of the twenty-first century. The project held in relative tension the mission to educate students for practical leadership, teach them to be theologians in residence, and provide them with a healing/redeeming/liberating experience.

The "God-Talk with Black Thinkers" project was launched in the fall of 2002 with Delores Williams, Carlyle Fielding Stewart III, Cheryl Kirk-Duggan, Karen Baker-Fletcher, and Gwinyai H. Muzorwa. This first intensive brought theologians and ethicists who applied their discipline to the needs of the worshiping communities. Since then, our intensive courses have been taught by Vincent Harding, Arthur Jones and Ferninand Jones, James Cone, Stacey Floyd-Thomas and Juan Floyd-Thomas, Zan Holmes, Carol Duncan, Alton Pollard, and Anthony Pinn.

## Semi-retreat Structure

The intensive, three-credit, elective course is offered by different guest lecturers each semester. We promote the retreatlike experience by limiting class size to twenty students. The class is provided at least one meal each day, thus encouraging students and guest faculty to eat together. Often, the dean and other Drew faculty will come and share in the meal. Worship is built into the schedule by the class attending campus worship; often the visiting scholar preaches in chapel.

This compact schedule assists students in ignoring the nonacademic distractions and resting from the responsibilities of their ministries and families. It is intended that this semi-retreat structure will become a luminous time in the life of students where they could learn and enter a period of self-discovery. The design of a retreat fosters the development of basic trust and knowledge of one another so that students and faculty might move toward becoming a community of scholars. In situations where we feel that a particular student cannot tolerate the intensity of this type of learning environment, we (after consultation with the dean) ask that the student not enroll in the courses.

*Invitation of Scholars*

A key, perhaps essential, element to the project is the guest faculty who are invited to mentor our students. *Mentoring* is perhaps a more accurate term than *teaching* for the work taken on by leaders of the intensives. Though there are many scholars' work to which we would want to expose our students, there are limited numbers of scholars whom we feel can create the kind of nurturing, pastoral ethos that is our priority. We do not want teachers who use tactics of shaming, humiliating, or blaming as teaching tools. We bring teachers who possess the ability to cultivate ideas, and, as important, teachers who embody transforming, compassionate leadership. We seek teachers who will model liberation theology, redeemed pedagogy. In short, we expose our students to mentors who have a passionate love of Black people. Cornel West, and many other educators, emphasizes the importance of having the structure and experience of any institution match the content of what is being communicated in the classroom—and vice versa. Consequently, students desiring to learn about liberating theology need teachers who can give them a liberating educational experience. As human beings we are our experiences. This requires that the faculty needs to be available for our students spiritually, socially, emotionally, and intellectually. It is never enough to simply communicate ideas in the God-Talk classrooms. Compassion for our students, a commitment to justice, and a desire to make the classroom the beloved community has to be demonstrated in every aspect of the faculty's work. We invite scholars who are people of faith with active relationships to worshiping congregations. We want to model to students that faith and intellect are not antitheoretical. We want to provide conversations that will assist seminary students who will combat the anti-intellectualism that plagues many of our churches and denominations. We seek scholars who will be invested in the personal and professional development of the students, in addition to being concerned for their mastery of the academic materials. We invite scholars who use a variety of teaching methods that we feel will educate the heart, soul, as well as the mind of the students. This has included the use of music, movies, art, worship, discussion, dance, and a variety of other methods of engagement. When there are colleagues whose work we want to bring to our students, but with whom we are not personally acquainted, we make every effort to check their references in terms of their ability to relate genuinely and warmly to students. We want academic rigor as well as passionate commitment of Black culture and Black students brought into the classroom with kindness and compassion. The scholars whom we invite must have a vitality that inspires students to want to know more, question deeper, and act with greater courage to make significant change in the churches and neighborhoods where they will serve.

When we invite scholars to teach in the project we simply tell them that they may teach whatever they want to teach. We suggest that they teach their most recent work, their most passionate ideas, and their "best stuff." Although we do not tell them what to teach, we are very careful to interpret our expectations and goals for the experience through which they will be guiding the students. We have crafted a detailed letter that describes the project.

We have several conversations answering questions and making plans. We feel that teachers are at their best when the subject matter is not dictated. We encourage guests to be creative, even unorthodox, in our classrooms.

## Public Forum

Each guest scholar is asked to give a public presentation of their work in the course to the seminary community. Some choose to give public lectures, others preach or perform some kind of artistic/musical liturgy in chapel. Some of the presentations have been part of the Theological School's major lecture series, such as Martin Luther King Day celebrations, while others have been simply held as a separate lecture series. In each case, the wider community seems transformed by the quality and depth of the presentation. The infusion of multiple Black intellectual voices into the larger seminary community has served to inform, inspire, and challenge the entire community, both faculty and students alike. It appears that the diversity of presentation is critical, reflecting the diversity of Black intellectual thought. Our hope is that this challenges the seminary faculty to include more Black scholars in their syllabi and course discussions. Our hunch is that the public aspect of the project has served to argue the importance of the project to the overall theological enterprise.

## Experimentation—the Evolving Model

We began the project by convening a kind of mini-conference. Our mini-conference entailed inviting five scholars over three days to do two lectures each. We quickly abandoned this style as it was too labor intensive. Next, we thought it important, early on in the project, to model for students familial collaborations. We wanted students to see, firsthand, families of scholars working together. To that end, we invited Art and Ferdinand Jones, who are brothers. We invited RoseMarie, Vincent, and Rachel Harding, who are mother, father, and daughter. We invited Juan and Stacey Floyd-Thomas, who are husband and wife. Though we are still interested in familial collaborations, our attention has turned to collaborations of folks who are in writing projects together. We thought it would be helpful to the cowriters to coteach as a way of working through some of their ideas.

There have been several delightful surprises along the way thus far. Stacey Floyd-Thomas has taught with the project twice and has brought students from Brite Divinity School. As a result of this, we have begun an institutional affiliation between Brite Divinity and Drew Theological. We cotaught a course in Ghana, West Africa, in January of 2006 with both Brite and Drew students enrolled in the course. Another unexpected benefit of the project has been the ongoing networking with project faculty. We are able to be in sustained conversations with those persons who have participated in the project. The network that has developed has been tremendous. Students from other schools—such as Emory, the University of Chicago, and Harvard—are now petitioning Drew for enrollment in the God-Talk courses. Our hunch is that Drew students are recruiting their friends from other schools to the courses.

## PART 3: CONTEXTUAL LEARNING THEORY: INCARNATIONAL APPROACHES AND ENGAGED PEDAGOGY

*Contextual Learning Theory*

There are a variety of approaches and uses of contextual learning theory in educational arenas. It is widely used in field education, cross-cultural education, clinical psychology, and other disciplines. For our reflection, we have used contextual education as the theoretical foundation upon which to design the God-Talk project as a liberative model of education. For our purposes, contextual learning, utilizing principles of engaged pedagogy and an incarnational-redemptive approach, assumes that education must assist students to be a liberating force in their communities. Contextual learning demands teaching for integration and congruence. The teacher's task is to make every effort to create an experience of congruence between the content of the material being taught and the method by which the class goes about analyzing the material. Additionally, the teacher is also charged with assisting students in their ability to see basic principles and concepts and the multiple and complex ways those concepts make connections. For example, in talking about racism, students must be able to see the multiplicity of definitions, experiences, and outcomes of racism.

Teaching for congruence and integration is critically important because there is a direct correlation between how students are taught in the classroom and how they go about ministry. For example, teaching students to be prophetic entails more than talking about the nature of the prophetic. From this perspective, the student must experience in the classroom a sense of their own ability to be prophetic, to be prophets. The experience of self in the classroom as prophet assists the student in wrestling with self-identity and in formulating a leadership role and responsibility in the local church. Experience, then, is not only what the student brings from beyond the classroom but is simultaneously what is happening in the classroom. The classroom then becomes the place where students experience and reflect upon all of experience. It is after reflection on these experiences that students are able to consider how to effectively transfer this experience to other environments, that is, the local church. Creating and maintaining classes that are integrative of a student's culture, history, tradition, and politics while at the same time creating conversations that are congruent is difficult but doable. Even though the experiences in God-Talk are brief, we assume that the intense retreat design and the feelings of being part of a community of scholars have lasting influences on the students and the rest of the seminary community.

*Engaged Pedagogy: The Practice of Freedom*

The God-Talk project is a model of engaged pedagogy. Engaged pedagogy has its philosophical roots in the theories reflected by bell hooks in *Teaching to Transgress*.[1] Dr. hooks writes that teaching at its best is the practice of freedom. Leaning heavily upon the work of Paulo Friere,[2] hooks defines engaged pedagogy as a sacred act where teacher and learner, together, strive in search of life-changing and life-affirming truth. As co-learners or partners, both the teacher and the student have passion to teach and learn, motivating each other toward transformation. While transformation is likely to occur individually and personally, the aim of engaged pedagogy is social transformation, social redemption, and societal healing. Engaged pedagogy teaches to challenge the status quo of society that would keep students passive and teachers bored and underappreciated. It also teaches to inform students to resist the societal thus educational domination by raising issues of race, class, gender, and sexuality as critical, foundational categories in all conversations. Engaged pedagogy encourages the experience of embodiment, that is, persons bringing all of who they are to the learning moment—body, mind, and spirit. The classrooms of engaged pedagogy are places that perpetuate the idea of teaching and learning as ecstasy, risk taking, and joy.

## Praxis

Black seminarians, particularly those attending white seminaries, do not have the luxury of a course of study that contains significant conversation about the practical knowledge needed for Black church leadership. A seminary curriculum steeped primarily in white church practices and traditions will not prepare a Black pastor for an adequate or competent career in the local church. Furthermore, with the urgency of the twenty-first century—with new forms of old racism, renewed U.S. global supremacy and imperialism, and the seemingly unending appeal of domination on all levels of U.S. society, while the population of the poor is increasing—neither do Black seminarians have the luxury of completing an MDiv degree that is not steeped in critical thinking, theological reflection, and intellectual rigor. Black seminarians need a course of study in seminary that is balanced in and integrative of theory and practice for justice while taking the needs, eccentricities, particularity, and complexity of Black culture seriously.

As an engaged pedagogical model, the God-Talk project leans heavily upon the notion of praxis to strengthen Black seminarians for local church leadership. Praxis involves the integration of both theory and practice for justice. Praxis teaching is teaching action and reflection upon action with the agenda to change the world for liberation of all peoples—both the oppressed and the oppressors. The courses engage in deep and significant dialogue, integrating issues of practice and theory that reflect the particular needs of Black people in a racist world. The conversations have a particular grounding in Black social, cultural, historical, and spiritual reference. God-Talk, with the aim of praxis, introduces or reintroduces Black students to ideas of African American scholars and the achievements and mistakes of exemplars as a way of preparing church leaders for thinking through and doing innovative leadership in the twenty-first century. In other words, praxis brings the task of problem solving for the survival and hope of an oppressed people into the classroom and challenges the students, teachers, and subject to speak to genuine situations of hurt, harm, and danger. Students report that the experience of praxis in the classroom in and of itself is liberating, transforming, and redemptive. Students having experienced in the classroom moments of grace, mercy, insightful ahas, healing, and joy-ringing hallelujahs can now replicate, duplicate, or envision anew these experiences of praxis in their parish settings.

## Role of Teacher/Role of Learner

Engaged pedagogy postulates that rather than students being passive recipients of the teacher's ideas, learners are expected to question, think critically, wonder, be curious, and hone intellectual rigor and creativity. In turn, teachers are also active learners who are striving to deepen and broaden their own experiences. Teaching recognizes that the world is multicultural and requires learning, unlearning, and relearning in ways that challenge domination. Learners come to the teaching enterprise not as blank slates or with blank minds but with a wealth of experiences, perspectives, and knowledge in order to passionately and critically engage in dialogue with the teacher, other learners, and the subject. Engaged pedagogy leads to self-actualization by requiring emphasis on the well-being of the oppressed as well as the well-being of the oppressor. Teacher and learner alike are asked to risk vulnerability as all are responsible for the conversation and for participation in the conversation. In other words, teachers and learners risk sharing the power of the learning process.

## Sense of Community

Education as the practice of freedom establishes intellectual community in the classroom where the participants, teachers and learners all, are passionate and willing to be deeply influenced and significantly changed by one another and the subject. Each guest professor in all the courses, as a way of modeling the value of each individual student and as a way of setting the expectation that each student must fully engage in the conversation, begins each course with extensive time for introducing himself or herself and invites each student to introduce himself or herself. These introductions announce to the students the expectation of full participation and risk taking. By asking students to introduce themselves to one another and to the guest faculty, a collective agenda declares that anonymity and passivity will not build a cohesive thinking community.

Community building is critical in engaged pedagogy as all the participants in the classroom are required to speak and listen and dialogue. This expectation not only builds community, but it also makes learning risky and uncomfortable. The risks of learning are both heightened and lessened when done in community. Risk is heightened when persons have the experiences of accountability and responsibility for their thoughts and actions. Risk is lessened when mistakes, experimentation, and new ways of thinking are considered part of the function of members of the intellectual community and are affirmed. Engaged pedagogy seeks to create a learning community where every voice is recognized and valued, and the students use their own voices strategically to speak, critique, and analyze. It espouses that learning is process-oriented and understands that the means of new thinking are just as important as the acquisition and demonstration of new thinking.

## Knowledge—an Expanded Definition

With mistakes, experimentation, and new ways of thinking as critical ways of being in the classroom, knowledge is not static, not based in data, facts, and memorization. Neither is knowledge out of reach of the learners, only the possession of the teacher. Knowledge includes the lessons of the classroom, the experiences of life, and the wisdom of tradition. Knowledge includes, but moves beyond, the traditional canon of information traditionally accepted by scholars. Critical thinking includes and trusts intuition, hunches, and gut reactions, just as it depends upon proven theory and traditional practice. This expansive definition of knowledge means that multiple perspectives are honored and affirmed in the classroom as new learning and new thinking take place. Engaged pedagogy seeks critical awareness through body, mind, and spirit. It promotes engagement of self, God, and neighbor for a holistic practice of learning. Challenging the dualism of the traditional banking system of education that is disembodied, engaged pedagogy restores the importance of subjectivity to the classroom experience. In the God-Talk classrooms, knowledge of folkways or cultural wisdom of the church mothers is not seen as "extra" or as an anecdotal appendage to the conversation.

Personal experiences of faith, awareness of God's activity in the community, and the wisdom of the ancestors are viewed as primary sources and necessary fodder in conversation.

## The Classroom

Engaged pedagogy assumes that the classroom is the place where students grapple with the issues that have seized our communities and that threaten to annihilate the present generation. The pedagogy strives to link the social, theological, and emotional with the cultural, economic, and political aspects of Black life. The classroom is not viewed as somehow being cloistered "away" from the community but, instead, seen as a place that is part of the community and responsible to the community. The classroom does not "become relevant" in engaged pedagogy. Instead, by grappling with the needs of the community with members of the community as teachers and learners, the classroom is a place where the relevant dialogue becomes deeply meaningful and germane to issues of survival and hope. In other words, engaged pedagogy espouses that in order for education to have liberating possibilities for the world, the world must be brought to bear on the classroom—pushing, stretching; creating doubt, confusion, surprise; and sparking deep, meaningful conversation. The community is significantly influenced by the classroom as the intellectual and theological ideals, morals, mores, values, beliefs, practices, and history of the community are all part of the educational enterprise through conversation, critique, and renewed vision. Engaged pedagogy takes seriously the understanding that the survival and health of the entire community are tied to its ability to shape the education of future generations.

## Language

Language is a powerful tool or weapon and can be used to dominate or liberate. Because conversation, thinking, and dialogue are considered the responsibility of all in the classroom, the use of "the king's English" is not considered to be critical, nor is it required. Students are encouraged to speak and write in the vernacular of their own choosing for their own comfort in expressing their own ideas. The elitism of Western culture and the superiority of the "well-educated" upper class is called into question when persons are given the freedom to speak as they know without being penalized, punished, or stigmatized. The community is charged to learn the vernaculars of those who are part of the community as a gesture of affirmation and willingness to admit that culturally influenced language possesses insight and wisdom that may not be translatable and perhaps should not be translated. Students moving from voiceless to voiced do not have to strain to communicate in an English that is the language of the oppressor. The use of vernacular frees up the listener and the speaker to communicate in authentic ways. While dialogue across differences and across boundaries creates opportunity for challenging bias and moving toward new thinking and new ideas, the dialogue must remain framed in words, phrases, and idioms that are meaningful to the one who is speaking the thought.

## Inherently Political

Engaged pedagogy for Black students is creating classroom experiences that acknowledge the inherent spiritual and political nature of education and that slant the political agenda of these classes toward the enrichment and liberation of African American peoples and the African American church. Teaching and learning are never politically neutral, racially neutral, gender neutral, or sexually neutral. In this approach, teaching and learning are inherently political enterprises having implications for every aspect of the community, that is, home, business, church, mosque, government, jail, and the marketplace. Black students do not need to employ a double-consciousness[3] in the classroom as their single-consciousness, in its complexity, is fully acknowledged, represented, and respected. An example of the political nature of teaching occurred midway though a seminar on ethics. During one of the seminar breaks, a Black student went to the university snack bar to get a sandwich (a fuller account of this incident appears in chapter 6). The student felt that she was treated improperly by a Hispanic employee and concluded that race was the reason for the mistreatment. The student returned to the classroom and reported the incident to the class and guest professors. Without hesitation, the guest professors integrated analysis and action of the incident into the course. As a living case study, the incident became the focus of the lesson for the next four hours and expanded to include the dean and her office personnel to arbitrate the racial offense with the cafeteria employee and the cafeteria manager. Had this not been an engaged pedagogical classroom, the experience of the student would have been discarded in the conversation as a typical racist occurrence and the class would have returned to "more important" work. As an engaged classroom, the incident was connected to and folded into the conversation and into the work of the classroom community. This connection moved the classroom out into the larger seminary, bringing the dean, her staff, and the cafeteria staff into the classroom as teachers and learners and problem solvers.

## Incarnational-Redemptive Approach

The incarnational-redemptive approach to the God-Talk project has three major assumptions. First, Black church studies programs and theological education must be places where students can discuss their racial identity in relationship to their anticipated professional roles. This approach views the formation of racial identity and professional roles as corporate processes that require the formation of a community. Second, it recognizes the reality of "gloss" in the African American Diaspora. *Gloss* is a psychological term that means diversity that exists within all communities. This approach avoids any essentialist definitions of Blackness. It emphasizes multiple, even contradictory, definitions and insists that the complexity of the community be reflected in every aspect of the learning experience. Third, the primary reason students choose ministry as a vocation is their desire to redeem the communities and individuals. As discussed in the section on engaged pedagogy, it is essential, then, that students experience redemption in the classroom setting if they are to bring healing and salvation to others.

### Racial Identity: Understanding Ourselves as Black People in a White World

The incarnational-redemption approach of the God-Talk project assumes that education must begin with an understanding of the humanity of the student. This requires that students have an opportunity to explore their personal and professional identities. Incarnation suggests that every aspect of the seminarian's life must now be part of the learning process for analysis as well as serving as a resource for theological reflection. For Black students this means the discourse must explore the experience of living in a racist world, for example, living with the experience of life in a color caste system. For women, the experience of gender discrimination must be part of the conversation. For Black students born outside of the United States, issues of immigration are critical. In short, Black students are no longer the other but are normative to the educational enterprise. The conversations of the classroom reflect the normativity of the student.

With this incarnational-redemptive approach we created a model where students could reconsider the meaning of living as Black people in a racist world. This educational enterprise embodies the soul of liberation theology. The point of departure for liberation theology is the life and existential condition of African Americans. For much of their academic life, African American students are rarely treated as subjects who shape discourse and determine the parameters of intellectual debate. In the God-Talk project, unlike typical education, African American students are treated as subjects. They are treated as persons of value with a vibrant intellectual and philosophical tradition and are encouraged to respond to one another as subjects rather than objects of curiosity.

In addition to exploring Black identity through conversations about the multiplicity of ways of being Black, male and female, the Project models the complexity of Blackness by presenting course materials through artistic expressions including popular culture, as well as through the rich variety of faculty teaching in the project. This diversity of identity is carefully represented in the faculty who are at times composed of husband-and-wife teams, brothers, fathers and daughters, and male-and-female teams. This display of diverse teaching teams, that is, diverse in ways of living and working as Black people seeking the liberation of Black communities, provides ample opportunity for students to experience the complexity of Black identity.

Second, the incarnational-redemptive approach to the God-Talk project means that we take seriously the issue of gloss. The concept of gloss acknowledges that multiple definitions exist for what it means to be African American, and that ethnic groups are composed of multiple smaller communities. Gloss recognizes that these smaller groupings redefine and challenge previous assumptions about the nature and character of any ethnic or social group. The notion of gloss is concerned with the harm caused when people feel they are excluded by others' definition for their ethnic or social group. Thus, debates about who is Black enough or who is an Uncle Tom or Oreo are avoided when the concept of gloss is made operative in Black church programs. For African Americans, this reality acknowledges that some families have had graduates from Harvard Medical School for three generations, while there are other families who have been in housing projects for four decades. In their own way, both are expressions of the African American experience in the United States. It is important to point out that most of the intellectual conflict with Black church studies and African American studies has occurred when people have felt that they have not been included in others' definition of "Blackness."

Much of the challenge lies in the theoretical problem of "gloss" in that no two African Americans would agree to the meaning of being African American or to an appropriate representation of the community. For example, there was considerable debate about the use of the movie *Rize* by David LaChapelle and the movie *Hustle and Flow*. Some students argued that each film, respectively, was not a worthy reflection of the Black community. Some students were concerned about the use of profanity and the lack of strong moral messages. Some students went so far as to say these movies should not be viewed in a seminary context. As a contextual course, based on the life of African Americans, much of the discussion centers around definitions and framing of the ontological notions of being African American.

For these reasons, it is crucial for us that no static or monolithic definition of "Blackness" shape the God-Talk project. In designing the God-Talk seminars, scholars are chosen who understand and represent a varied and at times conflicting understanding of the African American experience. We are intentional to include scholars who were born outside of the United States and who come from diverse theological, academic, social, and religious backgrounds to engage students about African American life.

And last, the incarnational-redemptive approach assumes that all learning must bring to focus the individual's social and cultural world, appreciating its embeddedness with other cultural worlds in a continuous flow of reciprocal and mutual influences. This means that Black church studies is forced to ask questions not only about the health of the African American community but also about the health of its relationship with the larger white community. This incarnational-redemptive approach to learning assumes that theoretical separations among social, individual, and corporate worlds are viewed as false dichotomies. Put in theological terms, we seek to create a structure that understands learning as redemptive and incarnational so that our students might be nurtured as creative leaders in multiple worlds.

For our purposes, redemption is understood as reconnecting people to their immediate social world and their wider communities. Within this framework, brokenness or "sin" does not suggest a state that exists within the individual but rather points to the unrelatedness and alienation of peoples and communities. One of the many aims of the God-Talk seminars is to reaffirm individuals' connection to their social groups (e.g., the Black community) and to understand and transform relationship with the wider society in and beyond the United States. Redemption!

# IN CONCLUSION

We wanted to re-create educational opportunities for Black pastors that would assist them in thinking about their identity as leaders and provide a model that would inspire seminarians to rethink the ministry and mission of the Black church in the world today. The structure of this course is designed to teach students how to theologize and work contextually. This approach to learning does not eliminate education's traditional focus of teaching students to think critically; rather, it contextualizes learning and thinking. The problem with classical educational theory is not its focus on memorization, the banking of cultural values, or the diverse social values competing for the minds of students. The problem is the inability to recognize that learning is a social process. It is a social process that requires community, social and cultural context, where people consider their action within this complex matrix of values and identities. As social beings we exist within a nexus of living systems and are profoundly context dependent in every aspect of our lives. We understand this process to be the essence of contextual education.

# RESPONSES

# Teaching Black, Talking Back

## Carolyn M. Jones

What "happens" when a Black body enters the class-room space? So much of the research on teaching and learning and on diversity concerns making the class-room a safe space for *students*, but as the chapters in this vol-ume have demonstrated, the classroom is not always a safe space for the teacher. Therefore, generating the conditions for learning becomes a very difficult task. The classroom has become a space that better reflects American culture—and this is a good and a bad thing. We have moved from educating priv-ileged "gentlemen" to preparing a diverse group of Americans for their role in participatory democracy. But this raises new issues. Charles H. Long writes:

> Since the 1960's, we have been confronted with a quite different situation in the discussion of liberal education. The fact that thou-sands of students graduate from high school without knowing how to read or write is an indication of the meaning that education now has in American culture. It is clear that several of the former gaps and distinctions are no longer present; and where such junctures are present, they are located in different places. For example, the gap defining the physical space of the university as separate from the urban space of its patrons and clients has changed: these phys-ical spaces now merge and interpenetrate, destroying the symbolic space of knowledge as reflection and leisure on the one hand, and a haven for a certain class on the other. The present continuity of

spaces presents us with the necessity of finding a concomitant meaning of knowledge within our society.[1]

That more traditional understandings of education have been replaced by a sense of education as professional training and as involved with "big sports," Long continues, shows us that the "university as an institution in American society is caught up in the communicative, informational, and material randomness of our culture."[2]

The Black body of the professor is situated at this juncture of change. The African American person signifies certain things in our current cultural configuration—significations inherited from our collective past and sent forward by cultural forms and norms. As Toni Morrison shows us in *Playing in the Dark: Whiteness and the Literary Imagination*, the cultural image of the African American was formed in slavery: "Nothing highlighted freedom—if it did not in fact create it—like slavery."[3] Black, bound, savage, exotic, and sexual—all these are things that the "new" Americans desired not to be.

The freedom of the "new" American—of the resurrected European, as Morrison puts it, utilizing and complicating W. E. B. DuBois' notion of "double consciousness"[4]—generated its own shadow side and projected that image outward, onto Blackness. The autonomy and individualism, authority, newness, and distinctiveness of the American was worked out in relation to the perceived "rawness and savagery" of Africanism.[5] Thus, the African came to "carry" the shadow: "to be the metaphor for transacting the whole process of Americanization."[6] Blackness, however, is not a pure binary; it is the other, unacknowledged and complicated self. Individualism "fuses with"[7] solitariness and alienation; newness and authority become a form of absolute power that is romantic, unwilling to reflect on action and repent, and that is wielded over the lives of others. Distinctiveness becomes difference—and who is more "other" than the African American except, now, the Mexican American and other Latino American?

The racialized body takes on a fusion with which it is difficult for the human being to live. Blackness is understood as both evil and protective, rebellious and forgiving, fearsome/repulsive and desirable/full of love—in short, it can carry "all the contradictory features of the self."[8] Morrison argues that, carrying all this, the Africanist presence "explodes" texts; in a similar way, the Black professor explodes the space of the classroom. As many of these essays state, the Black professor is, perhaps, the only experience of Blackness in the classroom that the students will have in a particular college or university. And that presence—which has authority—has to be controlled, minimized, silenced, and/or rewritten in order to be experienced "safely."

This is not only psychological process. We must not forget that the fusion that Morrison describes has, as she puts it, "ideological utility"[9] and market value. To the second: John Edgar Wideman in *Hoop Roots* talks about the image of Michael Jordan in American culture. Blackness, he writes—from minstrel shows[10] to Michael Jordan[11]—has fueled desire and created national style, and, in doing this, has become marketable and been used to accelerate globalization.[12] In a darker way, Morrison reminded us of the ideological and market's utility of Blackness in her work on the O. J. Simpson and the Clarence Thomas and Anita Hill cases. Under the "spectacle," the commodified story[13] is a cultural one, a metanarrative of "violence, class, race, capitalism, the control and distribution of information, equitable justice, constitutional guarantees, privacy, [and] patriarchial power"[14] linked to the metanarrative's subplot of Blackness as deviance.

Therefore, as a young gang member, hanging tough, once told my husband, then a police and gang officer, a "nigger" can always "click"—go off, turn on you, go wild: show the hidden (understood culturally as "true") nature beneath the mask of civility.

As Morrison reminds us, in discussing both Simpson and Thomas/Hill, the opposites that Blackness carries, in the metanarrative, can be "read" by others at any moment in the way that the young gang member suggested. Blackness can move from good to evil in a heartbeat, and those perceiving that change do not "need any logical transition from one set of associations to another."[15] Therefore, O. J. Simpson can move from his role as "affable athlete/spokesperson" to being "wild dog"[16] in a moment, without "any gesture toward what may lie in between the conclusions, or any explanation of the jump from puppy to monster"[17]— except the cultural understanding of "the general miasma of black incoherence."[18] Add to this the titillating possibility of "the unprecedented opportunity to hover over and to cluck at, to mediate and ponder the limits and excesses of black bodies"[19] that these public spectacles present, and the narrative of Black difference is complete. The Black body is racialized, as Stephen Ray puts it,[20] and eroticized, as Carol Duncan reminds us.[21]

So, in the classroom, the Black body is located, not just at a crossroads, dealing with the devil, but in a tangle of cultural ideas—what Mary Louise Pratt calls a contact zone—the threads of which, whipping about, sting like a lash.[22] To those we teach, therefore, we are both titillating and tricky, safe and potentially nurturing and threatening. We are either terrifying or entertaining. American culture educates us to expect "authentic"—read, "safe"—Blackness to come in only a few forms. If one is not athlete, hip-hop artist, comedian, or gang member, he or she is not "authentically" Black.

This extends to the classroom—and to our African American students too. Dr. Reggie Young, in a funny but very poignant paper called "Once I Was a Baby Raised in Blackness; or, Why Can't My New Millennial Cool Mo Black Students Pass a Simple Quiz in African American Studies?" given at the College Language Association Conference in Athens, Georgia, in April 2005, described how his African American students did not see him— someone steeped in the 1960s civil rights movement and the Black Arts Movement—as "authentically" Black. He lacked "cred," and African American students openly challenged him and his Blackness in class. I was interested and horrified to hear his experience echoed in the question-and-answer period of that session, which became a sharing of stories, among a predominantly African American group of professors, of outrageous disrespect.

Add to this that we are teaching religion. As Charles H. Long points out, the teaching of religion brings with it a number of problems. First, Long says, religion is "the only subject matter that is not in continuity with other forms of subject matter in previous secondary education. . . . For the most part, [students'] notions of religion have never been subjected to any form of critical reflection."[23] Second, "the teaching and study of religion has a dubious career within the university community."[24] There was a legal fight to teach religion in public schools, and there has been confusion about what it means to teach religion since. Is it teaching historical information or are we interested in faith and values? And the question persists about whether religion should be taught at all. Third, Long argues, we, as religion scholars, in order to prove our validity and rigor, tend to reduce the meaning of religion to methods compatible with or taken from other disciplines, "thus losing anything unique that such study might have added to the meaning of the curriculum."[25] All this, Long concludes,

> has to do with even the stranger meaning that religion carries within the cultural context of the American constitution and culture. Constitutionally, we are a non-religious nation; culturally, we are a "nation with the soul of a church."[26]

Add to this the very limited notion of African American religions that most people have, whether we are teaching that subject matter or not, and another layer of expectation and complexity is added as we enter the classroom.

So the African American body, teaching religion, a problematic subject matter, is caught in a tangle of cultural signifiers. In so many ways, our task is, as Anthony Pinn put it, turning body to flesh,[27] moving from idea and misinformation to reality. Given all this, we are left with some difficult choices. Am I to educate my oppressor, my younger—and sometimes not so much younger—brothers and sisters? The whole damned culture? The work is exhausting. But that seems to be the job we have taken on as educators. In such a pedagogical action, the classroom cannot be "safe" in the sense that questions are made "easy" but rather in the sense that it may be a space in which we can expose tensions that we may come to engage imaginatively.

I have always believed that my goal is to teach for transformation, but I have been uneasy with that. Into what do I want to transform my students, and who am I to do this? Reflecting on the chapters in this volume, I have further thought through this problem. I realize I do not want to transform them *into* something but instead to set the conditions for their deciding what they want to be. In secret, of course, I hope they will become loving, open, critically thinking good persons and citizens, but, honestly, they do not have to. To this end, on my syllabus, I always put a set of norms. They involve coming to class, buying the books, food, and so on. But I also emphasize—strongly—behavior. My norms read:

> 1. At times, we will be talking about things that are different and that may seem odd or weird to you, in tension with your beliefs and ideas. Discomfort is to be handled with reflection, not with insult, indifference, and/or insolence. In plain language, inappropriate language—verbal and body—will not be tolerated.
> 2. Respect is the order of the day—for your classmates, for the professor, and for the subject matter.

I expand on this by saying that if we enter into insult, I am not the only one insulted. The important issue is community, the difference that is present in the community—temporary though it is—of the class. In a way, I am asking them to "practice" a virtue. C. S. Lewis said that learning virtue is playing the children's game "Let's pretend": Just pretend to do the good behavior and it will become a part of your character.[28] This is a reminder that virtue is action, not just thought, as Aristotle taught us.

I remind students that within the classroom, there are students who practice these "other" religions and come from these "other" cultures, who live right here in Georgia, and who have thought-out ethical and moral orientations. I also tell them that they will encounter this microcosm as they enter the macrocosm of the work and everyday world. One outcome of this is that the racial-ethnic students and those students who practice different religions often feel free to speak up. I was truly pleased when, in my last "Judaism, Christianity and Islam" class, a Muslim student and a Baha'i student felt welcome to talk about their practices, and the class was truly open and interested. I love those moments when I, essentially, disappear, and the students teach one another. Then, the classroom becomes the image of the world I hope for: one in which people can listen to one another, exchange what they know, and either change or—and this is okay—agree to disagree. What I hope is that they can either change or agree to disagree and still see that there are goals larger than personal choices—such as peace—at stake for which they can work together, despite their differences.

Imagining this is, at depth, my work. My area of specialization is arts, literature, and religion. I am a postmodern/postcolonial womanist literary theorist (a designation that once caused a colleague's jaw to drop). I am also a Roman Catholic. All these are interrelated, in my racialized body. I believe that narrative—myth, story, fable, and so forth—is a way, perhaps the most important way, human beings learn about their worlds and one another. Black people, I think, have always had to be postmodern and postcolonial in their thought because slavery is at the core of the creation of the modern, and a people could not overcome it—legally or spiritually—by engaging the modern completely on its terms. I am a womanist because womanist thought involves reason, but it also understands that we are more than reason. And womanist thought acknowledges those forms of preservation of meaning—such as quilts and gardens—that kept alive, as Alice Walker puts it, *the notion of song*,"[29] of freedom. All of these contribute to the way I think about religion: It involves what orients us as we move in time and space, as Long puts it, in relation to ordinary and extraordinary things, as Catherine Albanese adds.[30] Finally, my practice of Catholicism involves all of these. Catholicism has a scholastic tradition, a mystical tradition, a liturgical tradition, a bodily tradition, and so on: It has a mode of expression for all the different kinds of people who practice it. These practices have emerged, partly, as Catholicism has encountered (and not always peacefully) many cultures.

Given this convergence in me, I contend that we are persons with multiple dimensions to our identities. We are called to develop in ourselves and in our students a complex toolbox with which we can continue to imagine, out of that multiplicity, both individually and collectively, what is possible and necessary to make a just and peaceful world. We inherit a story (the metanarrative, myth, and culture), but we are writing one too, and to compose it well—to think critically about what we inherit and, not to discard it but to put it in tension with the metanarrative, to adapt it to the metanarrative, and so on—is our task and responsibility.

I want to suggest two principles that set the foundation—at least for me—in thinking about how to teach Black. My clarity about this has come in light of the chapters in this volume. These principles are the dignity of the human person and solidarity, both Black and Catholic principles. I venture these in recognition of the Catholic Church's *real* problems with issues of race, not to mention sex and gender, but in accord with Pope Paul VI's call to African Catholics to share their "gift of Blackness."[31] In 1984, Black bishops of the United States articulated the African American dimensions of that gift in "What We Have Seen and Heard."[32] All this is "where I am coming from" in the classroom, my sense of location in tradition and discipline, meeting in my racialized, woman's body.

Long offers a keen insight into thinking about religion when he introduces, at the end of his essay, the metaphor of exchange.

Working with Marcel Mauss and with cargo cults, he suggests that we are always involved in processes of exchange, with their variety of power valences and obligations. To extend Long's potent signification on "the market," I will say one should add to exchange images of transaction and conversion. As slaves, Black people were producers and product, items of exchange who were bred, bought, and sold, producers of goods for and themselves goods in transaction, and converters, through their work, of matter into desirable objects. Blackness as commodity is clear. Perhaps claiming and then offering Blackness freely—as one's own/what one owns—is one way to resist commodification: a way to put what I have seen and heard in tension with what my students have seen and heard. With a gift of Blackness and with what Blackness offers, I will begin.

From its African past, African American Blackness, the bishops assert, has many things to share with community, church, and self. First, African American spirituality is scripture-based, accepting the Bible's promise of liberation and freedom. This freedom entails a responsibility: opposing oppression, "for unless all are free, none are free."[33] As M. Shawn Copeland puts it in "Method in Emerging Black Catholic Theology," in affirming Catholic tradition and word, "black Catholic theology affirms the unity of the word and the world, 'the humanity of human beings in the incarnation of God.'"[34] Second, Blackness emphasizes the gift of reconciliation.[35] We are called to forgive and to reconcile, and true reconciliation can only come with true equality. The call to reconcile, therefore, is a call for justice that safeguards the rights of all and that demands respect for the persons and cultures of others. Third, Blackness is spiritual, and Black spirituality has four gifts: It is contemplative, holistic, joyful, and communal.[36] This community's "heart" is, fourth, family, and in the African tradition, that has always meant "the extended family." This means that Blackness, fifth, values life, welcoming children, whether "legitimate" or not, into family.

Finally, Blackness is ecumenical: We must expand the notion of "Black church."

Despite the failures of the church, there are two truths that hold, I think, for all Catholics, and the bishops' statements reflect this in a Black way. First, we are communal people: Catholic identity is deeply liturgical, located in the public work for/of/from the people. This means that the ideal of solidarity is key. And, second, being Catholic involves the whole self—body (being and action), mind (thought and imagination/creativity), and spirit or heart (love, but heart is the seat of being as well)—as that "self" grows and changes from conception to natural death. This means that (ideally) Catholics start with and yield to the dignity of and charity toward the human person. Toinette M. Eugene suggests, given this Catholic orientation, a mediating term between ortho*doxy* (right thought or teaching) and ortho*praxy* (right action): ortho*pathy* ("righteous heart or feeling").[37] Such a triangulation strikes me as very womanist and postmodern, as well as very Catholic, refusing to be caught in a binary. In tension with the binary, Eugene asserts that we are more than body and mind; we are heart and spirit as well. As Long points out, this is also the issue in teaching religion, one of the *"human modes of thought that are of ultimate importance but may be more or less than reason."*[38] This is the basis of the dignity of the human person and of solidarity.

The divine image is present in every human person, but God, as a friend of mine expressed it once, "kneels at the altar of human freedom." That is to say, "The *right to the exercise of freedom*, especially in moral and religious matters is an inalienable requirement of the dignity of the human person."[39] We are embedded human beings, however; we are not fully self-sufficient. We can corrupt our own freedom and do harm to the neighbor, through unjust economic, social, political, and cultural conditions, such that the human person cannot achieve beatitude, that is, happiness.

Therefore, there "is a *solidarity among all creatures*,"[40] We are interrelated and interdependent. We are that extended family of which the Black bishops wrote, and this interconnectedness extends to all creation. Because of this, solidarity is not just a fact but a demand: It is part of what it means to be a human being. Solidarity is manifested in a just society in "distribution of goods and remuneration for work."[41] Therefore, it presupposes working for social justice and working against, as all the great liberators did, *anything*—social class, religious orientation, and so on—that divides us:

> Socio-economic problems can be resolved only with the help of all the forms of solidarity: solidarity of the poor among themselves, between rich and poor, of workers among themselves, between employers and employees in a business, solidarity among nations and peoples. International solidarity is a requirement of the moral order; world peace depends in part upon this.[42]

Solidarity also means sharing spiritual goods. This does not only mean spreading the faith, though that is part of it; solidarity means that we all come up together. As Pope Pius XII wrote, sharing spiritual goods means that we must urge others toward "the heroic charity . . . of [becoming] liberators . . . healers . . . and messengers . . . for the sake of creating the social conditions capable of offering to everyone possible a life worthy of a [human being]."[43] Generating this everyday heroism is what it has meant to me to "teach for transformation."

In the classroom—and this may be partly a function of getting older and meaner—more and more, I just refuse: I refuse to be minimized, reinterpreted, and controlled. I am a tenured professor who is well published and who thinks deeply about and loves the study of religion, and I strive to be a decent human being. That person is whom students encounter. When my people became objects of exchange in (the) America(s), that transactional culture began a process of exchange that created a nation—nay, a hemisphere and, perhaps, a world. This exchange is ongoing, and I am a product, yes, but also an authoritative agent of it. My insistence on this fact, on owning the variety and complexity of my identity, can make for some uncomfortable moments in the classroom. "A Black woman cannot . . ." some statements begin. But this insistence, as hardheaded as it sounds, is my way of offering my Blackness, my freedom, back, as a gift—and, in a sneaky way, of generating transformation and conversion. There are days I do not feel like giving anything, and there are days when the misunderstandings of my students may seem purposeful and pointed—and, as we have seen in these chapters, downright mean. But, at those times, certain voices call to me:

> You get your education, and *nobody* can *ever* take that away from you.
>
> —Katie Mae Jeffries, my grandmother

> You have been bought and paid for, and, now, you are free.[44]
>
> —Maya Angelou, one of my inspirations

> If there is one thing I am *radical* about, it is freedom.
>
> —Charles H. Long, my teacher[45]

> The promise of the gospel is not liberation, but freedom.
>
> —Gilbert I. Bond, my friend[46]

> We hold these Truths to be self-evident, that all Men are created equal, that they are endowed, by their CREATOR, with certain unalienable Rights . . . Life, Liberty, and the Pursuit of Happiness.
>
> —"Declaration of Independence," my country[47]

> Lord, by your cross and resurrection,
> you have set us free.
>
> —Memorial Acclamation, Roman Catholic liturgy, my church[48]

The beauty of interdependence is exemplified in this chorus of which I am a part and that is a part of me. The voices—some I love, some I resist—meet in me, and I sing out, against all that would diminish me, who, what, and where I am: strong, Black, female, and free.

# Together in Solidarity

## AN ASIAN AMERICAN FEMINIST'S RESPONSE

### Boyung Lee

Professor Lee, you look so nice today. I love your skirt! Did you change your hairstyle? You look more attractive with that style!" As I was getting the classroom ready, setting up high-tech equipment, I heard these comments. As I turned around, I found a middle-aged African American male student from another member school of the Graduate Theological Union (GTU) smiling at me. Later I learned that he was formerly an army GI who had been stationed in Korea for a short period of time. Evidently, he had had minimal interactions with Korean women while there and was unaware about our pedagogical protocols and our expectations about how faculty interact with students.

As I puzzled over how to respond, another voice chimed in indignantly, declaring, "I cannot believe you said what you just said. She is your professor!" It was a white woman student. She took it upon herself to speak for me. She often sweepingly referenced the rest of her imagined world—in this case, one including me—as the voiceless. So now she apparently intended to "save" her voiceless Asian American woman professor from a "sexist" male student.

The above incident illustrates my day-to-day experiences as an Asian American woman professor, teaching in a white liberal theological institution. Like many other Asian American women scholars, my authority as a teacher is complicated by the sexualized racial stereotypes and racialized gender stereotypes[1] that my students bring to the classroom. Moreover, as a feminist liberationist educator who esteems education as the practice of freedom,[2] I address straight on in the classroom the complicated and multilayered power dynamics of culture. This can lead, for instance, to questions about how to challenge students' sexualized and racialized notions about their Asian woman professor, and about how to establish my authority as a feminist liberationist teacher. How does one metamorphose one's classroom into a place where students become agents of transformation, moving beyond grotesque oversimplification and its attendant indignation, to living as radical visionaries?

As I read these thought-provoking essays, there was great resonance between these scholars and me: African American and Asian American theologians and religious educators are in mission together, and we need to remind each other of the wise teaching of African American ancestors, namely that "I am because we are." Our work for justice pivots on our interdependence and our mission to liberate all the cosmos and its members.

# THE PRETENSE OF POLITENESS: A ROOT CAUSE OF THE CURRENT RACE DISCOURSE

To frame discussions of the intertwinement of racism, sexism, classism, imperialism, and other forms of oppression in my class, I often share my experience as a woman who has recently immigrated. I sum up the current mainline approach to race as the pretense of politeness.

I moved to the United States fifteen years ago as an international student to pursue my call to ordained ministry, a call that I first noticed at thirteen, but one that I could not fulfill in my homeland because of my sex. Within ten days of my arrival, classes began. Until then, I had had little opportunity to speak English; but all of a sudden I found myself in a foreign country adjusting to a new culture, life, and language. My life was hectic, and it was full of constant challenges. Among many new things that I had to learn quickly was that, even though life at times was rough, when someone asked me how I was, there was only one response: I was expected to say, "Fine!" On the other hand, I am from a Confucian culture, one where, if one did not have time to visit, one would simply say "Hello!" and continue on one's way. Thus when I say, "How are you?" I really mean just that: that "I am here to listen to your story!" But in this country, no matter what was going on in my life, whenever I was asked how I was, I was always expected to say, "Fine!" If I expressed my real feelings, people were clueless about how to respond.

During these fifteen years, a lot has happened: a divinity degree, a PhD, a marriage, ordination, and a professorship. However, this "How are you?" "Fine!" formula still bothers me, and I sum up this aspect of American middle-class culture as a pretense of politeness.

I am deeply concerned about this pretense of politeness because, in my opinion, it is a serious problem that hinders American theological and religious education from being faithful to its call and mission. This pretense of politeness appears to be inclusive, but it really is a mechanism for sidestepping real issues, and thus it helps the powerful maintain the status quo.

In higher education, this pretense of politeness often takes the form of academic tokenism. For example, bell hooks says,

> All too often we found a will to include those considered "marginal" without a willingness to accord their work the same respect and consideration given other work. . . . What does it mean when

a white female English professor is eager to include a work by Toni Morrison on the syllabus of her course but then teaches that work without ever making reference to race or ethnicity?[3]

We observe many similar instances in theological and religious education. Imagine, then, theological and religious education scholars, students, and ministers trained by professors who have no time for race or ethnicity in the classroom. What kind of race discourse will their students facilitate in their own classrooms and parishes? It is my experience that many "liberal" scholars and students taught by such professors, those who speak from the perspective of the "other" and who criticize the reign of a white male-dominated theological center, actually contribute to marginalization. The white woman student described in the beginning of the essay is a good example. She easily spots gender-related issues but has no awareness of what her actions say about me racially. To speak for me, as though I am a bystander, is a serious form of racism and colonialism that many liberal white people indulge. Her action creates a dangerous situation, for it sometimes pits people from different minority groups against one another when this is not our reality. Defining *some* of many voices as "marginal" bespeaks tokenism, a mind-set that prevails in many theological and religious educational settings. Although the "other" has much to say about gender, race, religion, and economic status, a lot of liberal literature, including that of feminists, often portrays *others* primarily as oppressed victims, those who desperately need the salvation of the center.

Kwok Pui-lan observes that Chinese women, as described by Mary Daly, are passive victims to Chinese men's oppression. Daly's logic is that, since Chinese women cannot speak for themselves, Western feminists should save them from Chinese men.[4] Kwok points out that Daly's description of Chinese women is based on a Western colonial mentality; she misappropriates Chinese women in her effort to posit universal patriarchy. Thus, Daly overlooks Chinese women's role in history, both their shaping of it and their resistance to patriarchy. Native American religious scholar Laura Dolandson brings a similar analysis to Katherine Keller's work,[5] and Musa Dube, a postcolonial feminist biblical scholar from Africa, comments on the work of Elisabeth Schüssler Fiorenza.[6] In sum, some of these approaches to other-ness are based on tokenism and a Western colonial mentality that trivializes diversity while— at least in current discourse—pretending to celebrate it.

Sadly, when such tokenism is welcomed and celebrated by the "other" in the name of multicultural discourse, it can further marginalize people who are already marginalized. At the GTU, where I currently teach, there were about 134 full-time faculty members teaching at 10 different member schools as of the end of 2005. About 54 of them were women, and I was the only woman of color on tenure track; that is, until two of my colleagues were hired this year, one by my own school. As the heretofore only full-time woman of color on tenure track at the GTU, I am often asked to represent the marginalized at official and nonofficial functions. Obviously, my ethnicity or accent represents the collective consciousness of nonwhites to whites. There is an irony though, for even though I am now in the center in many ways, I am expected to speak from/for the margin. I call this situation a sweet and dangerous place. It is a sweet place because it makes me feel important and special. But it also is a dangerous place because I face the temptation to misappropriate or universalize others' stories for the sake of my specialness.

Whether we perceive ourselves to be at the center or on the margin, we live in multiple locations simultaneously. Being a professor at a major theological institution gives me authority and power that those on the margins do not have; this naturally puts me in the center. However, my experience as a Korean woman immigrant, one who speaks with a *strong* accent, constantly reminds me of my place in the margin of this country. Even in the Korean community, as a professor and as a clergyperson, I am typically at the center. At the same time, and as a woman in a

Confucian community, I am at the margin. My point here is that I live both at the center and at the margin, floating between the two, and creating other multiple locations on the way.

Despite the fact that I live in multiple locations, if I insist on having only one location—for instance, using my racial minority status to demand privilege, or by saying that I am a victim of sexism while concurrently ignoring my middle-class location, financial stability, and heterosexual married woman's privilege as conferred by culture—I arguably can advance my place in this hierarchical society at the cost of others. I see similar situations for many of my white women students: Because a lot of them are so focused on sexism in society and the church, they tend to ignore their own racist, classist, or imperialistic privilege. As an Asian feminist theologian, I often find it difficult to be engaged in serious dialogues with some of my white colleagues because they tend to see sexism as the only problem. As long as we keep this mode of thinking, teaching, and dialogue, the theological and religious education that we are engaged in will never transform the world.

Through my engagement with the African American male student I mentioned earlier, I discovered that he sees racism as the primary issue in U.S. society. Thus he fails to see sexism and other forms of oppression as serious problems. Therefore he intentionally and unintentionally participates in the perpetuation of the marginalization of women, especially women of color, by bringing sexualized racial stereotypes and racialized gender stereotypes to the classroom. In other words, this racialized convention, which is based on a pretense of politeness, coincidentally makes individuals insensitive to myriad power dynamics. And as this student's professor and as a fellow racial ethnic minority person, my task is to help students approach justice holistically: to see how racism, sexism, classism, colonialism, and other forms of oppression are imbued with power games, and thus to be sensitive to their interplay.

# PEDAGOGY IN SOLIDARITY TOGETHER

Rita Nakashima Brock, in a private conversation with me, said that the current mode of race discourse in theological and religious education assumes that there is one big circle and its center, with many small groups surrounding this big circle. Most of the time, small groups are only talking with the center, but they are not in conversation with any other small group in their neighborhood. Therefore, we often are competing with one another to be the privileged dialogue partner of the circle's center. However, if we are really serious about creating just theological and religious education, we should create a web of dialogue so that all of the groups are involved in multifaceted dialogue with one another, thus creating a dialogue of liberating interdependence. To accomplish this, I suggest that African American and Asian American theological and religious educators pursue the following.

First, we need to explore multidimensional hermeneutics through which our students from both centers and margins can be challenged and transformed. Onetime dialogue between two parties, the center and one of the marginalized groups, cannot accomplish just theological and religious education; rather, we need an ongoing conversation and praxis among all the parties, different cultures, and worldviews. For such a dialogue, we need to learn and relearn how to engage one another, face to face. As Audre Lorde says, "The master's tools will never dismantle the master's house."[7] For this, African American and Asian American theological teachers need to share our rich resources that we have inherited from our forbears. Together we should create new dialogical teaching and learning methods, ones that conjoin multiethnic, multireligious, and multicultural voices to highlight the plight of the oppressed, while challenging the center in the same breath.[8]

Second, we need to teach our students about the purpose of our work. Unlike the current discourse of race, the purpose of our dialogue and collaboration should not be inclusion or coexistence; rather, its purpose should be the liberation of those who are the most marginalized among us. When someone is suffering due to exclusion and oppression, how can one take seriously a purportedly multicultural church and academy? We need to ask Kwok Pui-lan's question: How much do our efforts contribute "to lessening human suffering; to building communities that resist oppression within the church, academy, and the society; and to furthering the liberation of those among us who are most disadvantaged, primarily women and the children"?[9] Another way of putting this is in the words of Nami Kim, a Korean American feminist theologian who teaches at a historical Black women's college, Spelman in Atlanta, who pointedly asks whether my/our comfort is gained at the cost of somebody else's.[10]

Third, we need to help our students examine critically and study the center. The above-referenced white student, for instance, should be encouraged to understand what it means to be white before she speaks for nonwhites. Strangely, even in the center there are subcenters and margins; however, in the current academic discourse about race, we typically "whitewash" the center as though we are all in agreement about who is there. White students need to raise questions about their identities as whites and the privileges that they have as white people. Helping them reflect on the contributions that they as white individuals can make to a multicultural community would be a good starting point. In a nutshell, talking about others without knowing oneself is nonsense.

Fourth, we need to teach our students, especially racial and ethnic minority students, to stop imagining nonexistent centers. As I suggested above, there are many subcenters within the center; however, when we assert one norm, then we effectively limit our contributions to multiculturalism, as though our own thoughts are afterthoughts. Then, rather than inviting diverse groups of whites to the roundtable, we turn to our neighbors sitting around the edge and grumble about the "center," thus allowing it to control our actions and to define us.

We need to reflect critically on who our conversation partners are, and why we tend to talk back to rather than talk with one another and the plurality of "centers."

Furthermore, together we need to keep revisiting our goals—our hopes and our dreams—lest they be lost to hand-wringing about the center. Trinh T. Minh-Ha, a postcolonial theorist, says that for some, difference means division. When we accept that argument, difference becomes a "tool of self-defense and conquest."[11] Thus the master calmly keeps her place at a nonexistent center while "others" foolhardily jockey to be nearby. When that happens, whether intended or not, we are trapped in that sweet but dangerous "special" place.

Looking at Blackness as the authors of this book do is not only an ongoing intra-communal project, as Juan Floyd-Thomas and Stacey Floyd-Thomas say in their chapter, but it is an intercommunal project. Hereto Asian American theological and religious educators are in solidarity with our African American colleagues—we are because you are!

# Influences of "Being Black, Teaching Black" on Theological Education

## Charles R. Foster

I n 1995 Rebecca Chopp explored "significant changes in theological education" due to the "dramatic rise in the number of women students" during the previous twenty years.[1] The writers of *Being Black, Teaching Black* extend the scope of her work. They illustrate the impact of Black faculty presence on the predominantly European American traditions of contemporary undergraduate and graduate theological education with examples from their own teaching practices.

I was asked in this essay to bring another perspective on the influence and impact of Black faculty on religious and theological teaching. In accepting this assignment, I have chosen to follow the example of the writers of the chapters. In the pages that follow, I explore the influence of Black faculty and students generally, and two colleagues in particular, in my own formation and practice as a white Anglo-Saxon Protestant theological educator.

I accepted the invitation to write this chapter, even though my experience as a white male teaching in U.S. theological schools for more than thirty years has been, in at least one way, somewhat unique. An African American religious educator introduced me

This essay is dedicated to Ethel R. Johnson and Grant S. Shockley, mentors in teaching Black and white.

to the practices of teaching. It happened this way. I grew up and attended college in the overwhelmingly white Pacific Northwest. At the same time, due to the work of my father and the attitudes of my parents, I had become sensitive to issues of economic and racial diversity in the community where I lived. Shortly after being admitted to New York's Union Theological Seminary for the fall semester of 1960, I was invited by the field education office to participate in an experimental program of field education supervision. That program began with a week-long laboratory school sponsored by The Methodist Church of Westfield, New Jersey, the congregational site of our field education experience. Our "laboratory leader" was Ethel Johnson. A product of Black Methodist congregations and schools in Staunton, Virginia, and New York City, a graduate of Bennett College and Hartford Theological Seminary, she was, at the time, a staff person for Christian education and camping ministries in the New York East Conference of The Methodist Church.

In the Methodist laboratory schools of the late 1950s and early 1960s, a group of adults as prospective teachers or "leaders-in-training" learned to teach by rehearsing several times over the course of a week the practices of planning, conducting, and evaluating teaching-learning sessions. They were guided in this effort by denominationally certified leaders such as Johnson. My fellow leaders-in-training included another student from Union and several volunteer teachers who would be teaching the junior-high youth in that congregation during the coming year. A group of fifteen to twenty junior-high youth participated in the sessions we planned for them each evening.

On the surface, the discovery methodologies and theories of John Dewey and other progressive educators dominated our learning and teaching during this five-day training program, but Johnson shaped our experience of that pedagogical tradition in a distinctive way. She guided us through collaborative exercises in which we *discovered for ourselves* patterns in adolescent learning, the relevance of the content and methodologies of the curriculum materials we had been given for the spiritual and intellectual development of the young people we were teaching, and the theological coherence and creativity of our own pedagogical proposals. She also led us in practices of praying for each other. She encouraged us to share our faith struggles with each other and she guided us as we read together biblical, theological, and educational texts for insight into what they might be saying to us and to the junior-high youth we were teaching.

This lab school, in other words, became for me an occasion to practice how to teach in the midst of the practice of being church for each other. Johnson had transformed both Dewey's methods of teaching and learning and the dialogue of prayer, Bible study, and daily life deeply rooted in the traditions of the Black church in her teaching. The interdependence of the academic and spiritual, the personal and communal, the immediate and historical that characterized the dialectic of theory-in-practice and practice-in-theory in her own teaching subsequently influenced my expectations of my education as a theological school student and later my assumptions about effective theological teaching. I discovered in this laboratory school experience a vocation I would later understand to be centered on theological teaching, and through Ethel Johnson, a welcoming community of Christian religious educators who embraced the vocational interdependence of the practice and scholarship of teaching.

Some ten years later, in the 1970s, Johnson and I were members of the same theological school faculty. In that school—due, in part, to the reputation of white faculty members deeply involved in the civil rights movement—the numbers of Black students had been increasing significantly. Their growing presence led to another significant influence on my teaching—one more explicitly focused on *what* I was teaching. The only way I know how to describe the source of that influence is to call it a collusion—a collusion both conscious and unconscious—of Black faculty and students. Black students were spending an inordinate amount of time in the offices of the three Black members of that faculty. In the safety of those offices these students could talk about what they were experiencing, share grievances, and seek suggestions for surviving spiritually and succeeding academically. More to the point, these Black colleagues helped them think strategically about how they might sensitize white faculty to the biases and prejudices in their teaching while expanding, at the same time, the consciousness of their white student peers to include perspectives and values deeply rooted in the Black cultural and religious experience. Many of those students returned to their classes prepared to challenge biases they encountered, ask questions that sometimes proved embarrassing, and suggest alternative and more inclusive ways to meet course assignments.

These same three Black faculty colleagues reinforced this consciousness-raising activity of Black students by challenging in faculty meetings the general lack of attention to the Black religious experience in the curriculum, the absence or marginalization of Black voices in course readings, the relevance of assignments for students preparing for ministries in Black congregations, and the omission of the traditions of Black worship in the seminary chapel. Through the years I have observed the transformation of the pedagogical cultures of other schools through similar patterns of collusion that challenge the hegemonic assumptions and practices of predominantly white and male faculty members. With hindsight, I realize that not all Black members of these faculties willingly embraced this role. Some actively resisted it. Many have shared their struggles with its impact on their time to prepare for teaching and do the research and writing they needed for tenure and promotion reviews. But the extent of their influence through those students in evoking changes in my teaching and that of many of our white colleagues cannot be underestimated.

I speak again from personal experience. Early in my teaching career a bright and thoughtful African American male student was the ringleader of a group of Black students who consistently enlivened discussions in class and then engaged me in private conversations about the work of the course. I knew he was spending considerable time in Ethel Johnson's office. I quickly discovered I could expect him to take the lead in expanding class discussions by asking questions grounded in his experience of the Black church and critiquing the readings I had assigned with insights from the early writers of the Black theology movement.

The impact on the future shape of my teaching was again profound. The inclusion of relevant readings and the use of case material from the Black religious experience, I soon decided, were not enough. Rather, after consulting with Johnson and several of these students, I recast a future class to put into dialogue Black and white perspectives on its primary topics. With that decision I discovered I could no longer assume that students and I shared a common cultural or religious frame of reference for reading a text or analyzing a problem or practice central to the educational goals that I, as teacher, brought to a course or class session. I eventually articulated this shift in my view of the interaction of teaching and learning in a somewhat facetious bit of copy for the school catalogue: "When teachers teach and students learn, students teach and teachers learn."

In the midst of these changing perspectives of myself as a theological teacher, I became acquainted with Grant Shockley who, at the time, was president of the Interdenominational Theological Center. I discovered he had been an important mentor and colleague of Johnson's. He was also an academic and ecclesial pioneer—one of those gentle persons who consistently turned upside down the racist patterns he encountered. He was a Black pastor in a predominantly white denomination, and the first Black member of the faculty at Garrett Theological Seminary and later at Candler School of Theology. He was often the lone voice of the Black church experience on numerous denominational and ecumenical boards and agencies. Several years of leadership in the office of missionary education of the denomination's Board of Missions introduced him to the freedom movements in Africa, Asia, and South America. A consummate bibliographer, he tracked down often deliberately obscured information to identify and make accessible resources that might help articulate a distinctively Black perspective on the academic and ecclesial discussions of theologians and religious educators. He became the second of my primary guides into the murky world of the interplay of Black and white theological teaching. Inevitably as we talked about some issue or gap in the literature over the course of several years, he would lean over to say, "And why don't you take on that project? Or organize that seminar?"

The resulting journey has been a lively one. I discovered new conversation partners as I took up one or another of those projects—in congregations, national church and ecumenical agencies, schools where I have taught, and among colleagues I have met through professional societies. Those conversations also directed my scholarly and pedagogical attention increasingly to the dynamics of power in racially, culturally, economically, and theologically diverse educational settings, the polyphonic shape of theological and ecclesial conversation that takes into account differences in the cultural contexts of our various religious journeys, and the holographic patterns to be found in the cultural and racial interactions of people in classrooms, institutions, and communities.

As I reflect on the influence, first of Johnson and Shockley, and later of my Candler School of Theology colleagues Luther Smith, Robert Franklin, Teresa Fry Brown, Noel Erskine, and Michael Brown, and of Black students throughout my teaching career, I realize that they also influenced how I *see* myself as a theological teacher. As we collaborated on essays, shared the tasks of our coursework, and worked together on faculty committees, I gradually realized I could not escape the messages conveyed by my "whiteness" to all students. That included those white students who viewed me as their racial, cultural, socioeconomic, and theo-logical ally and those students who viewed me as a stranger to their gendered, racial, cultural, socioeconomic, and theological experience and perspectives. It took longer, but through those conversations I also gradually discovered that both the burden and the gift of my "whiteness" could be an important resource for my teaching. That discovery, among other things, effectively decen-tered the social location of my teaching authority from the center to the periphery of the classroom. It meant becoming stranger to white students as well as to students from other racial and cultural backgrounds. It highlighted the value of collaborative teaching practices across the dynamics of our differences as a catalyst to the mutuality of our learning as teacher(s) and students. And it dram-atized the possibility that in the mutuality of teacher and student teaching and learning, we might all encounter the possibility of freedom from the hegemonic perspectives that hinder our ability to embrace the rich diversity of the human experience that lies in the multicultural, multiracial, multiethnic, and multireligious world that is the reality of the world in which we live.

Johnson and Shockley did not warn me that ambiguity is the constant experience of those who embrace the collaboration among Black and white teacher(s) and students or of any other forms of the diversity that make up the contemporary theological school classroom. But they did show me through their own teach-ing that some of the greatest surprises in learning and some of the most intense and powerful moments in learning communities emerge from the pedagogical embrace of the ambiguity that we experience in our interactions with one another. And for that I am most grateful.

# NOTES

## INTRODUCTION

1. Association of Theological Schools in the United States and Canada, www.ats.edu/resources/foliocol.pdf, "Diversity in Education" (accessed May 2, 2008). According to the Association of Theological Schools (ATS) statistics, in 2001, ATS schools were staffed by 200 African American faculty—an increase from 4 percent in 1980 to 6 percent in 2001 (242 reporting schools). The percentage of full-time racial ethnic faculty (i.e., African descent, Hispanic/Latino/a, Asian descent) in ATS-accredited schools rose from 4 percent in the fall of 1980 to 12.7 percent in the fall of 2001.

2. Ada Maria Isasi-Diaz's most influential titles include *En La Lucha/In the Struggle: Elaborating a Mujerista Theology* (Minneapolis: Augsburg Fortress, 2003); and *Mujerista Theology: A Theology for the Twenty-First Century* (Maryknoll, N.Y.: Orbis, 1996).

## 1. VISIBLE/INVISIBLE

1. Frantz Fanon, *Black Skin, White Masks* (New York: Grove, 1967), 110–12.

2. While my primary academic appointment is at a Canadian institution, I have served as a guest lecturer at postsecondary institutions in the United States as well.

3. Denise Taliaferro Baszile, "In This Place Where I Don't Quite Belong: Claiming Ontoepistemological In-Between," in *From Oppression to Grace: Women of Color and Their Dilemmas within the Academy*, ed. Theodorea Regina Berry and Nathalie D. Mizelle (Sterling, Va.: Stylus, 2006), 195–208.

4. Theodorea Regina Berry, "Introduction: What the Fuck, Now What? The Social and Psychological Dilemmas of Multidimensional Being as a Woman of Color in the Academy," in ibid., xiii.

5. Himani Bannerji, "Re:turning the Gaze," in *Thinking Through: Essays on Feminism, Marxism, and Anti-Racism* (Toronto: Women's, 1995), 97–119.

6. Carolyn Cooper, *Noises in the Blood: Orality, Gender and the "Vulgar" Body of Jamaican Popular Culture* (London: Macmillan Caribbean, 1993).

7. For example, the study of the music of Jamaican reggae superstar Robert Nesta Marley (1945–1981), more popularly known as Bob Marley. Reggae music emerged from the sociocultural context of urban Kingston, Jamaica, and was inextricably linked with the Jamaican phenomenon of the "rude boy" (young, urban, Black male youth who lived outside of the law) in the late 1960s. In the hands of Marley, however, the music became a tool for critiquing Jamaican colonial rule and espousing Rastafarian spirituality, philosophy, and ethics. As such, the study of Rastafarian religion and philosophy necessarily engages a music widely considered, in its early years, as "rude."

8. Baszile, "In This Place Where I Don't Quite Belong," 195–208.

9. Ibid., 199.

10. Ibid., 199–200.

11. Ibid., 200.

12. Ibid.

13. Ibid.

14. Ibid. In her use of the concept of "The Word," Baszile draws on the work of C. Lawrence, "The Word," in *Critical Race Theory: Key Writings That Formed the Movement*, ed. K. Crenshaw (New York: New Press, 1990), 336–54.

15. Baszile. "In This Place Where I Don't Quite Belong," 200.

16. Ibid., 201.

17. Sherene H. Razack, *Looking White People in the Eye: Gender, Race, and Culture in Courtrooms and Classrooms* (Toronto: University of Toronto Press, 1994).

18. W. E. B. DuBois, *The Souls of Black Folk* (New York: Penguin, 1996).

19. Ibid., 8.

20. Nancy Lynne Westfield, personal interview with the author, November 15, 2005.

21. Bannerji, "Re:turning the Gaze," 97–119.

22. Dorothy E. Smith, *The Everyday World as Problematic: A Feminist Sociology* (Toronto: University of Toronto Press, 1987).

# 2. USING NOVELS OF RESISTANCE TO TEACH INTERCULTURAL EMPATHY AND CULTURAL ANALYSIS

1. Mark Ellis and Richard Wright, "The Balkanization Metaphor in the Analysis of U.S. Immigration," *Annals of the Association of American Geographers* 88, no. 4 (Dec. 1998): 686–98.

2. Robert Carter, *Teachers College Record* 102, no. 5 (October 2000): 864–97.

3. Ngugi wa Thiong'o, *Petals of Blood* (New York: Penguin, 1977).

4. Nawal El Saadawi, *Woman at Point Zero* (New York: Palgrave Macmillan, 2005).

5. Ivan Turgenev, *Fathers and Sons* (London: Penguin, 1965).

6. James McBride, *The Color of Water* (New York: Riverhead, 1996).

7. Alice Walker, *Possessing the Secret of Joy* (New York: Pocket, 1992).

8. David Augsburger, *Pastoral Counseling across Cultures* (Philadelphia: Westminster, 1986), 69–95.

9. Ibid., 30.

10. Frantz Fanon, *Wretched of the Earth* (New York: Grove, 1963).

11. Margaret Kornfeld, *Cultivating Wholeness* (New York: Continuum, 2005).

12. Frantz Fanon, *Black Skin, White Masks* (New York: Grove, 1967).

13. William Cross Jr., Thomas Parham, and Janet Helms, "The Stages of Black Identity Development: Nigresence Models," in *Black Psychology*, ed. Reginald Jones (Berkeley, Calif.: Cobb & Henry, 1991), 319–38.

14. Robert Carter, *The Influence of Race and Racial Identity in Psychotherapy* (New York: Wiley, 1995).

15. Beverly Tatum, "Why Are All the Black Kids Sitting Together in the Cafeteria?" (New York: Perseus, 1999).

# 3. E-RACING WHILE BLACK

1. K. Anthony Appiah and Ann Gutman, *Color Consciousness: The Political Morality of Race* (Princeton, N.J.: Princeton University Press, 1996), 34.

2. *Oblivious* is a helpful term used by Mary McClintock-Fulkerson when describing the studied "innocence" of white persons involved with racial discourses.

3. Beverly Daniel Tatum, "Talking about Race, Learning about Racism: The Application of Racial Identity Development Theory in the Classroom," *Harvard Educational Review* 62, no. 1 (Spring 1992): 2.

4. James Davison Hunter, *Culture Wars: The Struggle to Define America* (San Francisco: Basic Books, 1991); *Before the Shooting Starts: Searching for Democracy in America's Culture War* (New York: Free Press, 1994); Mary E. Williams. ed., *Culture Wars: Opposing Viewpoints* (San Diego: Greenhaven, 1999).

5. Arthur M. Schlesinger, *The Disuniting of America: Reflections on a Multicultural Society* (New York: Norton, 1998), 86–87. While it is beyond the purview of this essay to critique all of the flaws that course through Schlesinger's argument, it is important to note his failure to apply the same methodological proviso to the construction of history by groups other than African Americans. Why, for instance, is it not necessary for any European cultural group to construct an intact genealogical chart as a basis for claiming a connection to "Western" culture—particularly given the historical reality that the fonts of Western civilization, Greece and Rome, considered much of what is present-day Europe barbarian and saw no connection to it? In fact, if one were to use the same stringent rule of geographic lineage that Schlesinger seems to apply to "Black" Americans, it is difficult to see how one could make sense of the idea of "Western" culture at all, given the diversity of language and custom that characterizes Europe. It would be difficult to make sense of, unless, of course, there is some implicit unifying principle. In this case, that unspoken principle is simply this: "Black" Americans are a people *sui generis*, therefore the principles that allow white Americans to identify a cultural connection to antiquity, no matter how strained, are inapplicable when dealing with Black history and culture.

6. Martin Bernal, *Black Athena: The Afro-Asiatic Roots of Classical Civilization* (New Brunswick, N.J.: Rutgers University Press, 1987); Mary R. Lefkowitz and Guy MacLean Rogers, *Black Athena Revisited* (Chapel Hill: University of North Carolina Press, 1996); Jacques Berlinerblau, *Heresy in the University: The Black Athena Controversy and the Responsibilities of American Intellectuals* (New Brunswick, N.J.: Rutgers University Press, 1999). As well, a brief perusal of website hits using the search terms "race" and "Egyptian" on Google makes this

point. There were well over twenty-five pages of links as of August 13, 2003, which debated this issue. What this demonstrates is that any assumption that the popular mind of most Americans, and, consequently our students, has freed itself from bondage to the ideological construction of Black origins is mistaken.

7. Beverly Daniel Tatum, "Talking about Race, Learning about Racism: The Application of Racial Identity Development Theory in the Classroom," *Harvard Educational Review* 62, no. 1 (Spring 1992): 2.

8. Judith Plaskow, *Sex, Sin and Grace* (Lanham, Md.: University Press of America, 1980); Valerie Saiving, *Woman Spirit Rising* (New York: Harper & Row, 1979).

9. Gustavo Gutiérrez, *A Theology of Liberation: History, Politics and Salvation* (Maryknoll, N.Y.: Orbis, 1988).

10. James Cone, *God of the Oppressed* (Maryknoll, N.Y.: Orbis, 1997).

11. Ibid.

12. Cecil W. Cone, *The Identity Crisis in Black Theology* (Nashville: AMEC, 1975); J. Deotis Roberts, *Liberation and Reconciliation: A Black Theology* (Maryknoll, N.Y.: Orbis, 1984).

13. This stumbling is not intended to diminish the value of works such as James Cone's, but rather to contend that if they are primarily used for "shock value" and no context is created for sustained engagement with the text, their pedagogical value is limited in significant ways. Not the least of which is that the Euro-American students, whether they experience alienation or catharsis in reading the texts, remain the primary beneficiaries of the conversation. Additionally, racial difference remains the grammar of the discourse, leaving the racialized imagination intact.

14. John Calvin, *Institutes of the Christian Religion*. 2 vols. (Louisville: Westminster/John Knox, 1960).

15. Augustine of Hippo, *Confessions* (New York: New City, 1997).

16. Reinhold Niebuhr, *Nature and Destiny of Man*. 2 vols. (New York: Macmillan).

17. The piece was used as a packet insert taken from *A Testament of Hope: The Essential Writings and Speeches of Martin Luther King, Jr.*, ed. James M. Washington. (San Francisco: HarperSanFrancisco, 1986).

18. Elizabeth Johnson, *She Who Is* (New York: Crossroad, 2002).

19. Howard Thurman, *Jesus and the Disinherited* (New York: Beacon, 1949).

# 4. CALLED OUT MY NAME, OR HAD I KNOWN YOU WERE SOMEBODY . . .

1. For more information on the social construction of whiteness, see Thandeka, *Learning to Be White: Money, Race and God in America* (New York: Continuum, 1999).

2. My colleague, Dr. Pam Holliman, executive director of Samaritan Counseling Center, Philadelphia, calls what I have labeled hallucinations as projection. Though I often resist the use of psychological categories in pedagogical reflection, I suspect she is right. The students are projecting their previous encounters and racist expectations onto me.

3. Candice M. Jenkins, "Queering Black Patriarchy: The Salvific Wish and Masculine Possibility in Alice Walker's *The Color Purple*," Modern Fiction Studies 48:4 (2002): 973.

4. Alton Pollard, "A Woman's Work, A Man's World: Critiquing and Challenging Patriarchy in the Black Family" (article presented at Black Theology and Womanist Theology in Dialogue, University of Chicago and the Lutheran School of Theology at Chicago, October 31–November 4, 2005), 17.

5. The original definition of *womanist*, coined by Alice Walker, appears in *In Search of Our Mother's Gardens* (San Diego: Harcourt Brace Jovanovich, 1983), xi.

6. While there is not time to unpack my incarnational pedagogy, I am aligned with such pedagogues as bell hooks, Paulo Freire, Thich Nhat Hanh, Parker Palmer, Anne Wimberly, Howard Gardner, and Katie Cannon.

# 5. READING THE SIGNS

1. See Mary Douglas, *Natural Symbols: Explorations in Cosmology* (New York: Routledge, 1996).

2. See Hortense J. Spillers, "Mama's Baby, Papa's Maybe: An American Grammar Book," *Diacritics* 17, no. 2. I am indebted to G. M. James Gonzalez's interesting discussion of this article. See note 3.

3. G. M. James Gonzalez, "Of Property: On 'Captive' 'Bodies,' Hidden 'Flesh,' and Colonization," in *Existence in Black: An Anthology of Black Existential Philosophy*, ed. Lewis R. Gordon (New York: Routledge, 1997), 130.

4. W. E. B. DuBois, *The Souls of Black Folk.* Library of America Edition (New York: Vintage, 1990), 7:

> Between me and the other world there is ever an unasked question: unasked by some through feelings of delicacy; by others through the difficulty of rightly framing it. All, nevertheless, flutter round it. They approach me in a half-hesitant sort of way, eye me curiously or compassionately, and then, instead of saying directly, How does it feel to be a problem? . . .

5. See Frantz Fanon, *Black Skin, White Mask* (New York: Grove, 1967), 116.

6. See Anthony B. Pinn, "Black Theology, Black Bodies, and Pedagogy," in *Cross Currents,* fiftieth anniversary issue 50, nos. 1–2 (Spring/Summer 2000): 196–202.

7. DuBois, *The Souls of Black Folk,* 8–9.

8. Ida B. Wells Barnett, *On Lynching: Southern Horrors, a Red Record, Mob Rule in New Orleans* (New York: Arno, 1969); *Without Sanctuary: Lynching Photography in America* (Santa Fe: Twin Palms, 2000).

9. See, for example, the photographs by Charles Moore at www.kodak.com/US/en/corp/features/moore/mooreIndex.shtml (accessed May 2, 2008); and *Eyes on the Prize* (New York: PBS Home Video, 1986).

10. See, for example, the following videos: *Divine Horsemen: The Living Gods of Haiti* (New York: Mystic Fire, 1987); and *Voices of the Orisha* (Berkeley, Calif.: Center for Media nd Independent Learning, 1993).

# 6. EMANCIPATORY HISTORIOGRAPHY AS PEDAGOGICAL PRAXIS

1. Carter G. Woodson, *The Mis-Education of the Negro* (1933; repr., Trenton, N.J.: Africa World, 1998), 53.

2. Ibid., 5.

3. Victor Anderson, *Beyond Ontological Blackness: An Essay on African American Religious and Cultural Criticism* (New York: Continuum, 1995).

4. W. E. B. DuBois, *The Souls of Black Folk* (1903; repr., New York: Oxford University Press, 2007), 37–38.

5. bell hooks, *Teaching to Transgress: Education as the Practice of Freedom* (London: Routledge, 1994), 7.

6. Ibid., 8.

7. Paulo Freire, *The Pedagogy of the Oppressed* (New York: Continuum, 1981), 22.

8. Ibid., 23–24.

9. Ibid., 30.

10. Ibid., 64.

11. Ibid., 67.

12. hooks, *Teaching to Transgress*, 13.

13. Freire, *The Pedagogy of the Oppressed*, 141.

# 7. BLACK RHYTHMS AND CONSCIOUSNESS

1. Vera Bell, "Ancestor on the Auction Block," in *West Indian Poetry*, ed. Kenneth Ramchand and Cecil Gray (Kingston, Jamaica: Longman Caribbean, 1971), 106.

2. These impulses gave rise to the voices of Caribbean figures such as Marcus Garvey who could challenge the prevailing assumptions of the Western world from a perspective that was self-consciously Black. See Michael Miller, www.cwmnote.org/papers.miller.htm (accessed March 15, 2006). Garvey was willing to have Caribbean people see God through the lenses of our own spectacles. See Garvey, *Philosophy and Opinions of Marcus Garvey*, vols. 1 and 2, 6th print., ed. Amy Jacques-Garvey (New York: Athenaeum, 1969), 44.

3. James Cone narrated his own experience in a lecture given at Fuller Theological Seminary (Pasadena, California, March 24, 2006).

4. Wilfred Cartey, in reviewing the work of Caribbean novelists, asserts that certain novels depict a system of education that leads to estrangement from the ritual of the folk and the rhythm of the land, and yet provides an impetus for the quest and eventual movement toward independence and self-determination among Caribbean people. See Wilfred Cartey, *Whispers from the Caribbean: I Going Away, I Going Home* (Los Angeles: Center for Afro-Caribbean Studies, University of California, 1991), xv.

5. Ibid., xiv.

6. Lucie Pradel, *African Beliefs in the New World: Popular Literary Traditions of the Caribbean*, trans. Catherine Bernard (Asmara, Eritrea: Africa World, 2000), xiv.

7. Dwight Hopkins, *Being Human: Race, Culture, and Religion* (Minneapolis: Fortress, 2005), ix.

8. Ibid., 119.

9. Ibid., ix–x.

10. Cornel West, *Prophetic Thought in Postmodern Times: Beyond Eurocentrism and Multiculturalism*, vol. 1 (Monroe, Maine: Common Courage, 1993), 5.

11. Anthony B. Pinn, *By These Hands: A Documentary History of African American Humanism* (New York: New York University Press, 2001), 4.

12. Cartey, *Whispers from the Caribbean*, xiii.

13. David Hume sets forth his views in his 1748 and 1754 essay "On National Characters." Quoted in Emmanuel Chukwudi Eze, *Race and the Enlightenment: A Reader* (Cambridge, Mass.: Blackwell, 1997), 33.

14. Others would build on Hume's work, and one such prominent figure is the German philosopher Immanuel Kant, who wrote "Observations on the Feeling of the Beautiful and Sublime" in 1764. He wrote,

The Negroes of Africa have by nature no feeling that rises above the trifling. Mr. Hume challenges anyone to cite a single example in which a Negro has shown talents, and asserts that among the hundreds of thousands of blacks who are transported elsewhere from their countries, although many of them have been set free, still not a single one was ever found who presented anything great in art or science or any other praiseworthy quality, even though among the whites some continually rise aloft from the lowest rabble, and through superior gifts earn respect in the world. So fundamental is the difference between these two races of man, and it appears to be as great in regard to mental capacities as in color.

Quoted in Eze, *Race and the Enlightenment*, 55.

15. Hopkins, *Being Human*, 7–8. Hopkins suggests that one becomes human "by gearing all ultimate issues towards compassion for and empowerment of people in structural poverty, working-class folk, and the marginalized."

16. Lincoln Galloway, "Black Hole, Luminescent Constellations: A Question of Authenticity" (paper presented at the American Academy of Religion annual meeting, San Antonio, Tex., November 23, 2004).

# 8. FROM EMBODIED THEODICY TO EMBODIED THEOS

1. Patricia Williams, "The Alchemy of Race and Rights" in *Law and Morality: Readings in Legal Philosophy*, ed. By David Dyzenhaus and Arthur Ripstein (Toronto: University of Toronto, 2001), p. 243.

2. This is a further nuancing of W. E. B. DuBois' notion of double consciousness. For his full definition, see W. E. B. Dubois, *The Souls of Black Folk*, Library of America ed. (New York: Vintage Books, 1990), 8–9.

3. The concept "Superwoman-Villian Dichotomy" comes from a pedagogical tool created by Katie G. Cannon, which she uses as a context for understanding womanist pedagogy and the challenges posed to the real-lived context of Black women's authority in the classroom and academy. I note, with appreciation, that this section is a narrative exemplification of her handout that outlines this phenomenon. I received the handout in a course with Dr. Cannon while her doctoral student at Temple University in 1999. The handout is unpublished and is entitled "The Black Woman as Intellectual: Super Woman or Villian."

4. hooks, bell. *Black Looks: Race and Representations* (Boston: South End Press, 1992), 21.

5. Katie G. Cannon, *The Womanist Theology Primer Remembering What We Never Knew: The Epistemology of Womanist Theology* (Louisville: Women's Ministries, Presbyterian Church U.S.A., 2001), 14–15.

6. Ibid., 15.

7. Ibid.

8. Michael Eric Dyson, *Is Bill Cosby Right?: Or Has the Black Middle Class Lost Its Mind?* (New York: Perseus Books Group, 2006), 31. For a fuller description and explanation of each of these stages, see chapter 3 of this text, pages 33–49.

# 9. TEACHING BLACK

1. bell hooks, *Teaching to Transgress: Education as the Practice of Freedom* (New York: Routledge, 1994).

2. Paulo Freire, *Pedagogy of the Oppressed* (New York: Continuum, 1981).

3. For further information on double consciousness, see W. E. B. DuBois, *The Souls of Black Folk*, Library of America ed. (New York: Vintage Books, 1990).

# 10. TEACHING BLACK, TALKING BACK

1. Charles H. Long, "The University, the Liberal Arts, and the Teaching and Study of Religion," in *Beyond the Classics: Essays in Religious Studies and Liberal Education*, ed. Frank Reynolds and Sheryl L. Burkhalter (Atlanta: Scholars Press, 1990), 32.
2. Ibid.
3. Toni Morrison, *Playing in the Dark: Whiteness and the Literary Imagination* (Cambridge, Mass.: Harvard University Press, 1992), 32.
4. Ibid., 44.
5. Ibid.
6. Ibid., 47.
7. Ibid., 45.
8. Ibid., 59.
9. Ibid., 64.
10. John Edgar Wideman, *Hoop Roots: Playground Basketball, Love and Race* (New York: Houghton Mifflin, 2001), 170.
11. Ibid., 40–41.
12. Ibid., 42.
13. Toni Morrison, "The Official Story: Dead Man Golfing, Introduction," in *Birth of a Nation 'hood: Gaze, Script, and Spectacle in the O. J. Simpson Case*, ed. Toni Morrison and Claudia Brodsky Lacour (New York: Pantheon, 1997), xxvii.
14. Ibid., xxiv.
15. Toni Morrison, "Introduction: Friday on the Potomac," *Race-ing Justice, En-gendering Power: Essays on Anita Hill, Clarence Thomas, and the Construction of Social Reality*, ed. Toni Morrison (New York: Pantheon, 1992), xv.
16. Morrison, "Dead Man Golfing," viii.
17. Morrison, "Friday on the Potomac," xv.
18. Morrison, "Dead Man Golfing," ix.
19. Morrison, "Friday on the Potomac," xvii.
20. See chapter 3 of this book.
21. See chapter 1 of this book.

22. See Mary Louise Pratt, *Imperial Eyes: Travel Writing and Transculturation* (New York: Routledge, 1992).

23. Long, "The University, the Liberal Arts," 35.

24. Ibid.

25. Ibid.

26. Ibid.

27. See chapter 5 of this book.

28. C. S. Lewis, *Mere Christianity* (San Francisco: HarperSanFrancisco, 2001), 187.

29. Alice Walker, "In Search of Our Mother's Gardens," in *In Search of Our Mother's Gardens* (New York: Harcourt Brace Jovanovich, 1983), 237. Italics in original.

30. Catherine Albanese, *America: Religion and Religions* (Belmont, Calif.: Wadsworth Publishing Company, 1981).

31. Jamie Phelps, "Black Spirituality," in *Taking Down Our Harps: Black Catholics in the United States*, ed. Diana L. Hayes and Cyrian Davis, O.S.B. (Maryknoll, N.Y.: Orbis, 1988), 196.

32. "What We Have Seen and Heard: A Pastoral Letter on Evangelization from the Black Bishops of the United States," 1984, www.aodonline.org/AODonlineSQLimages/Evangelization /seenandheard.pdf (accessed May 2, 2008).

33. Ibid, 1.

34. M. Shawn Copeland, "Method in Emerging Black Catholic Theology," in *Taking Down Our Harps: Black Catholics in the United States*, ed. Diana L. Hayes and Cyrian Davis, O.S.B. (Maryknoll, N.Y.: Orbis, 1988), 134.

35. "What We Have Seen and Heard," 1.

36. Ibid., 1–3.

37. Toinette M. Eugene, quoted in Copeland, "Method in Emerging Black Catholic Theology," 127.

38. Long, "The University, the Liberal Arts," 35. Emphasis in original.

39. *Catechism of the Catholic Church*, 2nd ed. (Washington, D.C.: United States Catholic Conference, 2000), §1738. The *Catechism* is cited by section number.

40. Ibid., §344.

41. Ibid., §1940.

42. Ibid., §1941.

43. Ibid., §1942.

44. Maya Angelou, "Million Man March Poem." www.empire zine.com/spotlight/maya/maya-p2.htm (accessed May 2, 2008).

45. Charles H. Long, personal conversation with author.

46. Gilbert I. Bond, personal conversation with author.

47. "Declaration of Independence," Archive of Early America, www.earlyamerica.com/earlyamerica/freedom/doi/text.html (accessed May 2, 2008).

48. *Let Us Celebrate!* ed. Maria Elena Rodriguez (Franklin Park, Ill.: World Library Publications, 2005), 126.

# 11. TOGETHER IN SOLIDARITY

1. K. Cho Sumi, "Converging Stereotypes in Racialized Sexual Harassment: When the Model Minority Meets Suzie Wong," in *Critical Race Feminism: A Reader,* ed. Adrien Katherine Wing (New York: New York University Press, 1997), 204–5.

2. bell hooks, *Teaching to Transgress: Education As the Practice of Freedom* (New York: Routledge, 1994).

3. Ibid., 38.

4. Kwok Pui-lan, "Unbinding Our Feet: Saving Brown Women and Feminist Discourse," in *Postcolonialism, Feminism and Religious Discourse,* ed. Laura E. Donaldson and Kwok Pui-lan (New York: Routledge, 2002), 69–75.

5. Laura E. Donaldson, "The Breasts of Columbus: A Political Anatomy of Postcolonialism and Feminist Religious Discourse," in *Postcolonialism, Feminism and Religious Discourse,* ed. Laura E. Donaldson and Kwok Pui-lan (New York: Routledge, 2002).

6. Musa Dube, *Postcolonial Feminist Interpretation of the Bible* (St. Louis: Chalice, 2000).

7. Audre Lorde, *Sister Outside: Essays and Speeches* (Trumansburg, N.Y.: Crossing, 1984), 99.

8. R. S. Sugirtharajah, *Postcolonial Criticism and Biblical Interpretation* (Oxford: Oxford University Press, 2002), 13.

9. Kwok Pui-lan, *Discovering the Bible in the Non-biblical World* (Maryknoll, N.Y.: Orbis, 1995), 31.

10. Nami Kim, " 'My/Our' Comfort Not at the Expense of 'Somebody Else's': Toward a Critical Global Feminist Theology," *Journal of Feminist Studies in Religion* 21, no. 2:75–94.

11. Trinh T. Minh-Ha, *Woman, Native, Other: Writing Postcoloniality and Feminism* (Bloomington: Indiana University Press, 1989), 82.

# 12. INFLUENCES OF "BEING BLACK, TEACHING BLACK" ON THEOLOGICAL EDUCATION

1. Rebecca Chopp, *Saving Work: Feminist Practices of Theological Education* (Louisville: Westminister John Knox, 1995), ix.

# SELECT BIBLIOGRAPHY

Adams, Michael Vannoy. *The Multicultural Imagination: "Race," Color, and the Unconscious.* New York: Routledge, 1996.

Altbach, P. G., and K. Lomotey, eds. *The Racial Crisis in American Higher Education.* Albany, N.Y.: SUNY Press, 1991.

Anderson, Victor. *Beyond Ontological Blackness: An Essay on African American Religious and Cultural Criticism.* New York: Continuum, 1995.

Anzaldua, Gloria, ed. *Making Face, Making Soul/Haciendo Caras: Creative and Critical Perspectives by Feminists of Color.* San Francisco: Aunt Lute, 1990.

Appiah, K. Anthony, and Ann Gutman. *Color Consciousness: The Political Morality of Race.* Princeton, N.J.: Princeton University Press, 1996.

Barnett, Ida B. Wells. *On Lynching: Southern Horrors, a Red Record, Mob Rule in New Orleans.* New York: Arno, 1969.

———. *Without Sanctuary: Lynching Photography in America.* Santa Fe, N.M.: Twin Palms, 2000.

Berlinerblau, Jacques. *Heresy in the University: The Black Athena Controversy and the Responsibilities of American Intellectuals.* New Brunswick, N.J.: Rutgers University Press, 1999.

Bernal, Martin. *Black Athena: The Afro-Asiatic Roots of Classical Civilization.* New Brunswick, N.J.: Rutgers University Press, 1987.

Berry, Theodorea Regina. "Introduction: What the Fuck, Now What? The Social and Psychological Dilemmas of Multidimensional Being as a Woman of Color in the Academy." In *From Oppression to Grace: Women of Color and Their Dilemmas within the Academy,* edited by Theodorea Regina Berry and Nathalie D. Mizelle. Sterling, Va.: Stylus, 2006.

Blauner, Robert. "Talking Past Each Other: Black and White Language of Race." In *Race and Ethnic Conflict,* edited by Fred. L. Pincus and Howard J. Ehrlich. Boulder, Colo.: Westview, 1994, 27–34.

Bowser, Benjamin P. et al. *Confronting Diversity Issues on Campus.* Newbury Park, Calif.: SAGE, 1993.

Butler, Johnnella E. "Transforming the Curriculum: Teaching about Women of Color." In *Transforming the Curriculum: Ethnic Studies and*

*Women's Studies*, edited by Johnnella E. Butler and John C. Walter. Albany: SUNY Press, 1991, 67–87.

Cho, Sumi, K. "Converging Stereotypes in Racialized Sexual Harassment: When the Model Minority Meets Suzie Wong." In *Critical Race Feminism: A Reader*, edited by Adrien Katherine Wing. New York: New York University Press, 1997.

Collins, Patricia Hill. *Black Feminist Thought: Knowledge, Consciousness, and the Politics of Empowerment*. 2nd ed. New York: Routledge, 2000.

Cone, Cecil W. *The Identity Crisis in Black Theology*. Nashville: AMEC, 1975.

Cone, James. *God of the Oppressed*. Maryknoll, N.Y.: Orbis, 1997.

Cooper, Carolyn. *Noises in the Blood: Orality, Gender and the "Vulgar" Body of Jamaican Popular Culture*. London: Macmillan Caribbean, 1993.

Delgado, Richard, and Jean Stefancic, eds. *Critical White Studies: Looking behind the Mirror*. Philadelphia: Temple University Press, 1997.

Derman-Sparks, Louise, and Carol Brunson Phillips. *Teaching/Learning Anti-Racism: A Developmental Approach*. New York: Teachers College Press, 1997.

Donaldson, Laura. "The Breasts of Columbus: A Political Anatomy of Postcolonialism and Feminist Religious Discourse." In *Postcolonialism, Feminism and Religious Discourse*, edited by Laura E. Donaldson and Kwok Pui-lan. New York: Routledge, 2002.

Dube, Musa. *Postcolonial Feminist Interpretation of the Bible*. St. Louis: Chalice, 2000.

DuBois, W. E. B. *The Souls of Black Folk*. New York: Penguin, 1996.

Ellis, Mark, and Richard Wright. "The Balkanization Metaphor in the Analysis of U.S. Immigration," *Annals of the Association of American Geographers* 88, no. 4 (Dec. 1998): 686–98.

Fanon, Frantz. *Black Skin, White Masks*. New York: Grove, 1967.

Fiol-Matta, Liza, and Mariam K. Chamberlain, eds. *Women of Color and the Multicultural Curriculum: Transforming the College Classroom*. New York: The Feminist Press, 1994.

Foster, Charles R., Lisa E. Dahill, Lawrence A. Golemon, and Barbara Wang Tolentino. *Educating Clergy: Teaching Practices and Pastoral Imagination*. San Francisco: Jossey-Bass, 2006.

Freire, Paulo. *Pedagogy of the Oppressed*. New York: Continuum, 1981.

Giroux, Henry. *Living Dangerously: Multiculturalism and the Politics of Difference*. New York: Peter Lang, 1993.

Gonzalez, G. M. James. "Of Property: On 'Captive' 'Bodies,' Hidden 'Flesh,' and Colonization." In *Existence in Black: An Anthology of Black Existential Philosophy*, edited by Lewis R. Gordon. New York: Routledge, 1997.

Graff, Gerald. *Beyond the Culture Wars: How Teaching the Conflicts Can Revitalize American Education*. New York: Norton, 1992.

Gutiérrez, Gustavo. *A Theology of Liberation: History, Politics and Salvation*. Maryknoll, New York: Orbis, 1988.

Himani Bannerji. "Re:turning the Gaze." In *Thinking Through: Essays on Feminism, Marxism, and Anti-Racism*. Toronto: Women's Press, 1995.

hooks, bell. *Teaching to Transgress: Education as the Practice of Freedom*. New York: Routledge, 1994.

Hunter, James Davison. *Before the Shooting Starts: Searching for Democracy in America's Culture War*. New York: Free Press, 1994.

———. *Culture Wars: The Struggle to Define America*. San Francisco: Basic, 1991.

Kim, Nami. "'My/Our' Comfort Not at the Expense of 'Somebody Else's': Toward a Critical Global Feminist Theology." *Journal of Feminist Studies in Religion* 21, no. 2 (2005): 75–94.

Lee, Boyung. "From a Margin within the Margin: Rethinking the Dynamics of Christianity and Culture from a Postcolonial Feminist Perspective." *Journal of Theologies and Cultures of Asia* 3 (March 2004): 3–23.

Lorde, Audre. *Sister Outside: Essays and Speeches*. Trumansburg, N.Y.: Crossing, 1984.

Minh-Ha, Trinh T. *Woman, Native, Other: Writing Postcoloniality and Feminism*. Bloomington: Indiana University Press, 1989.

Pinn, Anthony B. "Black Theology, Black Bodies, and Pedagogy." *Cross Currents*, Fiftieth Anniversary Issue 50, nos. 1–2 (Spring/Summer 2000): 196–202.

Plaskow. Judith, *Sex, Sin and Grace*. Lanham, Md.: University Press of America, 1980.

Pui-lan, Kwok. *Discovering the Bible in the Non-biblical World*. Maryknoll, N.Y.: Orbis, 1995.

———. "Unbinding Our Feet: Saving Brown Women and Feminist Discourse." In *Postcolonialism, Feminism and Religious Discourse*, edited by Laura E. Donaldson and Kwok Pui-lan. New York: Routledge, 2002, 69–75.

Razack, Sherene H. *Looking White People in the Eye: Gender, Race, and Culture in Courtrooms and Classrooms.* Toronto: University of Toronto Press, 1994.

Roberts, J. Deotis. *Liberation and Reconciliation: A Black Theology.* Maryknoll, N.Y.: Orbis, 1984.

Schlesinger, Arthur M. *The Disuniting of America: Reflections on a Multicultural Society.* New York: Norton, 1998.

Smith, Dorothy E. *The Everyday World as Problematic: A Feminist Sociology.* Toronto: University of Toronto Press, 1987.

Spillers, Hortense J. "Mama's Baby, Papa's Maybe: An American Grammar Book." In *Culture and Counter Memory: The "American" Connection,* edited by S. P. Mohanty. Special Issue, *Diacritics* 17, no. 2 (Summer 1987): 65–81.

Tatum, Beverly Daniel. "Talking about Race, Learning about Racism: The Application of Racial Identity Development Theory in the Classroom." *Harvard Educational Review* 62, no. 1 (Spring 1992): 1–24.

———. *Why Are All the Black Kids Sitting Together in the Cafeteria?* New York: Perseus, 1999.

Tusmith, Bonnie, and Maureen R. Reddy, eds. *Race in the College Classroom.* New Brunswick, N.J.: Rutgers University Press, 2002.

Westfield, N. Lynne. *Dear Sisters: A Womanist Practice of Hospitality.* Cleveland: Pilgrim, 2000.

Williams, Mary E., ed. *Culture Wars: Opposing Viewpoints.* San Diego: Greenhaven, 1999.

Woodson, Carter G. *The Mis-Education of the Negro.* Trenton, N.J.: Africa World Press, 1998. Reprint, Washington, D.C.: Associated Publishers, 1933.

# CONTRIBUTORS

Carol B. Duncan is Associate Professor and Chair of the Department of Religion and Culture at Wilfrid Laurier University, Waterloo, Ontario, Canada.

Juan M. Floyd-Thomas is associate professor of history at Texas Christian University, Fort Worth, Texas.

Stacey M. Floyd-Thomas is associate professor of ethics and director of Black Church Studies at Brite Divinity School at Texas Christian University, Fort Worth, Texas.

Charles R. Foster is professor of religion and education emeritus at Candler School of Theology of Emory University, Atlanta, Georgia.

Lincoln E. Galloway is associate professor of homiletics at Claremont School of Theology, Claremont, California.

Carolyn M. Jones (Carolyn Medine) is associate professor of religion and literature, African American religions and literatures, religious theory and thought, and women's spirituality and writings at the University of Georgia, Athens, Georgia.

Boyung Lee is assistant professor of educational ministries at Pacific School of Religion, Berkeley, California.

Anthony B. Pinn is Agnes Cullen Arnold Professor of Humanities and Professor of Religious Studies at Rice University, Houston, Texas.

Arthur L. Pressley is Associate Professor of Psychology and Religion at Drew University, Madison, New Jersey.

Stephen G. Ray Jr. is Jeremiah A. Wright Sr. Associate Professor of African American Studies and Director of the Urban Theological Institute (UTI) at Lutheran Theological Seminary, Philadelphia, Pennsylvania.

Nancy Lynne Westfield is associate professor of religious education at Drew University, Madison, New Jersey.